BAMBOULA AT KOURION: THE ARCHITECTURE

Area E from northeast, across House I.

UNIVERSITY MUSEUM MONOGRAPH 42

BAMBOULA AT KOURION: THE ARCHITECTURE

Saul S. Weinberg

Published by
THE UNIVERSITY MUSEUM
University of Pennsylvania
1983

Production
    Publications Division, The University Museum

Typesetting
    Deputy Crown Inc., Camden, N.J.

Printing
    The Sheridan Press, Hanover, Pa.

Library of Congress Cataloging in Publication Data

Weinberg, Saul S., 1911-
    Bamboula at Kourion : the architecture.

    (University Museum monograph ; 42)
    1. Bamboula Site (Kourion) 2. Architecture,
Domestic—Cyprus—Bamboula Site (Kourion) I. Title.
II. Series.
DS54.95.K68W44   1983   728′.0939′37   83-6596
ISBN 0-934718-36-9

IN MEMORY OF

JOHN FRANKLIN DANIEL

AND

JOE S. LAST

CONTENTS

CONTENTS

LIST OF ILLUSTRATIONS

Frontispiece.   Area E from northeast, across House I

FIGURES

PLATES

PREFACE

The late John Franklin Daniel excavated the Bronze Age settlement at Bamboula, east of the village of Episkopi in south-central Cyprus, beginning in 1937 and ending with his untimely death in 1948.[1] He published a preliminary report soon after the first season's work[2] as well as articles on some of the finds from the first three campaigns.[3] In two important book reviews, he gave concise outlines of his views on the stratigraphy of the Bamboula settlement.[4] The 1948 campaign was to be devoted largely to answering questions that had arisen while he was writing his text on the results of the three seasons of digging, 1937-1939. By that time, he had written a first draft describing most of the structures uncovered in the excavations and had revised some of the text on the basis of his latest findings; the text for Area A was the part most revised, that for Area E the part least revised. We shall follow Daniel's text, with minor revisions, except for Area E, where subsequent investigations have caused a fundamental change in our understanding of the architecture.

Shortly after Daniel's death, I was invited to complete the publication of the Bamboula settlement, but it was not possible for me to visit the excavations until the summer of 1951, when I did so with the aid of a grant from the American Philosophical Society. During that summer, Ellen Kohler of the University Museum assisted greatly in recovering all possible information from the excavation records. It was then decided that, in the limited time available to me, a thorough study of only the architecture of the site was possible, and the summer was spent in going over the records left by Daniel, in examining the plans on the site, in reading the text in so far as it had been completed, in investigating questions that Daniel had raised in marginal notes, some of which involved a small amount of digging, and in preparing new plans where necessary, especially restored house plans. The plans were all drawn by C. Polycarpou, under the supervision of the late J. S. Last of Episkopi. Some revisions to these plans, especially the addition of the 1954 excavation by J. L. Benson, have been made by John Huffstot, who has also done the drawings for Figures 7 and 12. The material presented here is, then, essentially the result of the work done in 1951, much of it involving only slight revisions in Daniel's text.

Any publication of the architecture was, of course, dependent on a study of the stratigraphy of the site, and of the finds. The stratigraphic study, together with the publication of the many tombs, was undertaken by Benson, who went to Kourion for the year 1953-1954. During the following year, he studied the Bamboula material in the University Museum, and for the first term of the 1955-1956 academic year he continued work on the project at the Institute for Advanced Study in Princeton. The results of his stratigraphic studies he very kindly sent to me in preliminary form between early 1956 and 1961, ten to fifteen years before they were published.[5] Unfortunately, I was by then so much involved in other research and publication that it was not possible for me to return to the Bamboula architecture until recently. In the meantime, a very short report of a paper read at the annual meeting of the Archaeological Institute of America in December 1951, was published,[6] and this served as the basis for a brief summary of the Bamboula architecture in the *Swedish Cyprus Expedition.*[7]

During my stay in Cyprus in the summer of 1951, I had most fruitful discussions with the late Porphyrios Dikaios on the Late Bronze Age architecture at Enkomi, where he was then excavating, and on comparisons with the architecture of Bamboula; the rectangular-tripartite house was found at both places. At the same time, Joan du Plat Taylor was excavating at Myrtou Pigadhes and, again, was most generous in sharing her material and her knowledge with me.

I should like to express a special debt of gratitude to the late George McFadden for the hospitality of Curium House during the summer of 1951. That summer I benefited greatly from conversations with J. S. Last, whose knowledge of the architecture of all aspects of the Kourion excavations was fundamental. The arrangements for the publication of the Bamboula architecture and for furnishing photographs from the archives at the University Museum have been made by G. Roger Edwards, who has kindly read the manuscript and made many corrections and suggestions. The text has also profited from the suggestions made by S. E. Iakovides after his reading of the manuscript. To the staff of the University Museum's Publications Division go my final thanks for the production of this volume.

SAUL S. WEINBERG

December 1978
Columbia, Missouri

---

1. Excavations were conducted as follows: 1937—March 1 to May 28; 1938—March 22 to June 10; 1939—March 20 to June 8; 1948—October 21 to November 23. In addition, Virginia Grace made soundings at the Circuit Wall during 1941, and J. L. Benson did a small amount of digging in Area E in 1954.
2. Daniel 1938. Very brief and general reports on this and the next two seasons appear in Daniel 1937, Daniel 1939b, and Daniel 1940.
3. Daniel 1939a; Daniel 1941.
4. Daniel 1943.
5. Benson 1969; Benson 1970; Benson 1972.
6. Weinberg 1952.
7. Åström 1972, 14-17.

CHAPTER I

INTRODUCTION

The excavations of ancient Kourion by the University Museum, under the direction of Bert Hodge Hill, began in 1934. Three years later, work started at the Late Bronze Age settlement on Bamboula, supervised by John Franklin Daniel, a member of the Kourion staff, who in his first report on the excavations described the site as follows:

> The Bamboula is the northern part of a low ridge which separates the river Kouris from the village of Episkopi. This ridge starts in the south, at the locality Phaneromeni, where there are traces of a settlement and necropolis of the Early Bronze Age, and runs northwest, crossing the Limassol-Paphos highway and culminating just south of the old Paphos road. It consists of a core of sandstone, broken up into many terraces. In places the rock is visible; in others it is covered by a fair depth of earth. The top of the Bamboula, some forty feet above the plain, is flat and covered with threshing floors. The Late Bronze Age tombs opened by the British Museum expedition[1] are visible on the outcroppings which outline the terraces of the west and northwest slopes. The Late Bronze Age city was found in a large field, which starts at the outcroppings below the summit, slopes down at an angle of six to ten degrees to an irrigation ditch, and then drops abruptly three meters to the plain. It faced the river valley, which must have

been an important highway, as well as the source of water. It is sunny in winter and protected from the prevailing west wind. It is steep enough for drainage and high enough for protection. The Bamboula commands the entire countryside.[2]

The contours of the ridge form a rough semicircle, with the highest point somewhat to the east of its center (pl. 1a). It is the center of the threshing floor at the very top of the ridge that was used as the datum point for the excavations, with all measurements taken below that point. The datum point is at 88.49 m. above sea level.

During the 1937 season, ten trenches were opened, usually measuring 10.0 by 2.0 m. or 10.0 by 1.5 m. Trenches 1, 2, 3, 4, 5 and 7, all on the northeast slope of the ridge and close to its lower edge, were later incorporated into Area A (fig. 1), one of the two large fields of excavation, which was dug in the following two seasons as well. Trench 6, begun in 1937 and continued in 1938, became Area F. Trench 8 was nonproductive, 9 crossed the line of the Circuit Wall and 10 connected 2 and 4. In 1938, besides continuing most of the trenches already mentioned, Daniel opened a long trench (11), originally 22.0 by 1.50 m., in a north-south direction at the top of the ridge to

---

1. Walters 1900.

2. Daniel 1938, 261.

1

the west of the threshing floor; this resulted in the discovery of the great stone-lined well, which became the focal point of Area B. Trench 11 was later extended to a length of 55.0 m. Trenches 15, 17 and 18 were in this same area; the last was nonproductive. Partly down the northwest slope, trenches 12, 13 and 14 were opened, to form Area C; Trench 12 was 18.0 by 2.0 m.; the others were smaller and parallel to it. Trench 16 was dug at the lowest part of the slope, almost directly west from the threshing floor and the well; when enlarged and further investigated it became Area D. Work in 1939 centered on the further excavation of the great well and the opening of a second large area, E, on the lower reaches of the northwest slope of the ridge. Trenches 19, 20 and 21 were the components of Area E (fig. 1).

When, after the long delay caused by service in World War II, Daniel returned to Bamboula in 1948, he cleaned up parts of Areas A, D and E, did some further digging at the Circuit Wall in Area A and investigated many small areas where he had questions about stratigraphy or architectural relationships. His work was by no means completed when he left for Turkey to participate in a survey being conducted for the University Museum, during which he met an accidental death.

A few short exploratory excavations completed the work on Bamboula: in 1941 Virginia Grace made soundings at the Circuit Wall in Area A at the request of Daniel. During my stay at Kourion in the summer of 1951, I conducted some small-scale excavations, mostly in Area A, with a view to elucidating points that Daniel had questioned, or which were not clear to me from his text. While J. L. Benson was working in Episkopi through the year 1953-1954, he carried out a brief exploratory excavation in Area E,[3] the results of which are incorporated in the plans presented here.

With respect to the present publication, it must be remembered throughout that we are dealing with an incomplete excavation. Daniel was in the midst of resuming his prewar excavations after nine years; he had only begun to clean, to probe, to investigate. For Area A, he had a revised manuscript as of June 1942, which he was again reviewing in the field. This is the area for which he

had come farthest in formulating his ideas concerning the architecture. The text we present is very largely his, with but minor variations based on our observations of 1951. For Area B, he left no text, and what is presented here is taken from the field notebooks. For Area C, which produced no architecture and proved to be exclusively of stratigraphic significance, the brief text left by Daniel has been published in Benson 1969, 16-19, and it need not be considered here. Daniel's text for Area D had been considerably revised and is accompanied by his plans for the houses. While there is a text for Area E, on which Daniel had done much work and had made many changes, it is full of marginal queries to which he was never able to give his attention. His plans for the houses are tentative and indicate that he was still looking for fuller and better interpretations. It was here that I concentrated my attention in 1951, which resulted in some interpretations quite different from those of Daniel, a different numbering of some of the houses,[4] and entirely new house plans in several cases. Because of the very tentative nature of Daniel's thinking about this area, which was certainly the most difficult one at the site due to the very thin and disturbed nature of the fill, I have felt free to present a text which is entirely my own. Daniel would certainly not have wished to have his text published as he left it; we would not do him this disservice. For Area F, there is too little recorded to make any publication possible; the architecture indicated on the plan is of little consequence.

Under the circumstances, in which the stratification of the settlement has been studied separately and fully published,[5] and the finds from the site are also published,[6] we have only to accept the published results and refer to them for the dating of the architecture in its main and subphases. In every case, reference is made to the pertinent publication. This has the great advantage of permitting us to concentrate on the presentation and analysis of the architecture itself and makes for brevity in our presentation.

---

3. Benson 1969, 22; Benson 1970, 33-34.

4. This problem is dealt with in some detail at the beginning of the discussion of Area E (see below, p. 36).

5. Benson 1969 and 1970.

6. Benson 1972. For all finds mentioned here, the catalogue number from Benson 1972 is given in parentheses immediately following, e.g., B621.

The absolute chronology adopted here, taken from Benson 1972, page 58, is as follows:

Late Cypriote IA:1	1600-1550
Late Cypriote IA:2	1550-1450
Late Cypriote IB	1450-1400
Late Cypriote IIA	1400-1350
Late Cypriote IIB	1350-1275
Late Cypriote IIC	1275-1225
Late Cypriote IIIA	1225-1100
Late Cypriote IIIB	1100-1050

One aspect of this publication in which the incompleteness of the excavations will perhaps be most obvious is the photographic illustration. While a full photographic record of the course of the excavations was made, and many of these photographs have proved useful in illustrating details in particular, the large area photographs that are usually made at the end of an excavation, specifically with the final publication in mind, are absent. It is my hope that the available photographs, together with the plan, will make possible an adequate visualization of the architecture by the reader.

CHAPTER II

AREA A

THE EARLIEST REMAINS AND STRATUM A

Area A comprises the regions excavated and recorded in the field records as Trenches 1, 2, 3, 4, 5 and 7 (fig. 1). Trench 1 was not carried to undisturbed levels; Trench 3 was early fused with 2; Trenches 5 and 7 are discussed separately under the heading Circuit Wall. In the preliminary report of the work of the first season (1937),[1] everything in Area A, Periods 1, 2, 3 and 4, corresponds to Strata D, E, F and G respectively in this final report.

The earliest remains discovered *in situ* in Area A, or anywhere on the site, for that matter, were those of a tomb of the Early Cypriote period which lay outside and partly under the Circuit Wall[2] (fig. 2, Tomb 1; and pl. 1b).

Traces of occupation of LC IA date were found in the corner formed by Rooms A.VIII.1 and A.VIII.3 (fig. 2, bottom) and in a pit just to the west of this at the edge of the excavated area (Benson 1969, 5, A:1; 1970, 25, A:1, and 40, LC IA:2).[3] The pit contained a pithos and a few sherds, presumably remaining from a house of the LC IA period (Benson 1969, 5, A:1).

Earth which appears to be deposit of this same period was found between −9.15 m.[4] and the bedrock in the eastern corner of the room. The pit was cut by the adjacent walls of the LC IIIB House A.VIII and could not be associated with contemporary structural remains. The only stratified levels on Bamboula earlier than this are Area C, Level A:1 and Area E, Level A:1, which are of a slightly earlier LC IA phase (Benson 1970, 40, LC IA:1).

The earliest consistent traces of habitation in Area A are those shown in figure 2. Although no walls were preserved, a series of cuttings and pits furnishes some idea of the nature of the buildings. The outstanding feature of the remains of this period is the large cutting in bedrock at *a.1, a.2* and *a.3*. In *a.1-2* the rock is cut away sharply to the northeast and northwest respectively; *a.3* is cut away to the southeast, leaving a deep channel between it and *a.2*. The sides of these cuttings were undoubtedly higher at the time of Stratum A, but were reduced in height when the rock was cut back in preparation for the houses of Stratum D. An artificial ridge, *b,* joins the eastern end of *a.1* at right angles. This cutting is less clearly defined than most of *a*, due no doubt to mutilation in

---

1. Daniel 1938.

2. Benson 1972, 10.

3. Wherever pertinent throughout the text, reference to the stratigraphy as published in Benson 1969 and 1970 will be given in this form.

---

4. All levels are given as below the datum point, which is at 88.49 m. above sea level.

4

subsequent periods. The area labeled *c,* below and enclosed by cuttings *a.1* and *b,* consists of the roughly smoothed bedrock, covered by an artificial fill—A2a (Benson 1969, 5, A:2a)—possibly a floor, consisting in part of stony earth and in part of clay. The rock appears in places. An irregular pit (Pit 1) and a larger depression to the northeast of it which was dug as a series of pits, contained a fill—A2b (Benson 1969, 5, A:2b)—differing from that of A2a. Perhaps this is material thrown in to level off natural depressions in the terrain, although it appears subsequent to Stratum A2a. Some 0.20 m. of ashy earth—A3 (Benson 1969, 5, A:3)—presumably accumulation, were found over A2a in *c.* This stratum runs to approximately the bend in cutting *a.1,* north of which its place is taken by less ashy earth. About 0.10 m. of brown earth—A4 (Benson 1969, 5, A:4)—which lay over Stratum B, perhaps remain from building debris of Stratum A. Whatever their exact nature, they are intermediate chronologically between A3 and Stratum B.

Two roughly circular pits were cut just inside and above the southeastern end of cutting *a.1;* three more ran down the center of *b,* and a sixth stood at the corner between these two rows. The pits were deep, obviously artificial, and contained small stones placed around their sides in a manner to indicate that they once held wooden studs in place. These studs would have run up the walls to give added support to the masonry. Those on foundation *a.1* may have been visible in the face of the wall, if its base is assumed to rest in the bottom of the cutting; the others were in the center of the wall on foundation *b* and would not have been visible. Similar construction will be noted below (pp. 37-38) in connection with Area E, House I, of the LC IA period. No such traces were found in the northwestern part of *a.1,* nor in *a.2* or *a.3.* This would seem to indicate that walls stood on *b* and at least the southeastern half of *a.1.* There seems no reason to doubt, however, that there were other walls on the remainder of *a.1,* and on *a.2* and *a.3.*

The large Pit 2 was found outside and partly under the Circuit Wall. This pit was filled flush with the bedrock surface with stony earth containing a considerable number of potsherds. Because the associated levels outside the pit were disturbed to bedrock in Roman times, it was im-

possible to determine the precise stratigraphical context of the pit. Since, however, the fill was similar in purpose to that of the depressions listed under A2b (Benson 1969, 5, A:2b), and since the pottery it contained was synchronous with that in those depressions, all have been grouped together under A2b. Pit 2 differs from the others only in that it was obviously artificial. In view of its shape, it appears probable that it was originally a tomb of the Early Bronze Age, comparable to Tomb 1. It would seem to have been standing when the rock was cut back prior to the construction of Stratum A, or perhaps still earlier, at which time it was cleared out and filled. Tomb 1 escaped detection at this time because it had already collapsed.

Bothroi of LC II date were discovered sunk into the bedrock under later remains in House A.V, Rooms 1 and 5—Bothroi 1 and 2—and House A.VI, Rooms 4, 5 and 6—Bothroi 3, 4 and 5 (see fig. 24). That they antedate the LC IIIA buildings is clear from the fact that most of them lie at least in part under walls of the later houses. The floors of the houses to which these bothroi belonged were destroyed prior to the construction of the LC IIIA houses, so that there is no architectural evidence to indicate to which of the LC II strata these pits belong. The pottery which they contained, however, indicates a date early in the LC II period, comparable to our Stratum A. The position of these pits, furthermore, is consistent with the house walls of Period A, which can be restored hypothetically on the basis of the cuttings *a.1-3.* Pit 4, under A.V.1, for instance, would occupy the corner of a room if the walls were 1.00 m. wide, a width which is suggested by the spacing of the post-holes in foundation *b.*

The well under A.VI.5 is only 3.10 m. deep and is now dry. The well on the top of Bamboula shows that water was available at a high level. The well under A.VI.5 was oval in shape and was furnished with footholds cut into opposite faces. It was filled with firm grey earth relatively free of stones and containing many potsherds, some from nearly whole pots. The lower part of the deposit was stratified in such a way as to indicate that it had settled in water. From the floor level of Stratum D to a point 0.80 m. down, the well was widened and disturbed when the houses of

Stratum D were built, perhaps in the hope of reusing the well. If so, the idea was abandoned and the opening was filled with stones and clay.

The lower part of Pit 3, under A.VI.4, was lined with clay, apparently the packing around a large storage jar which was removed subsequently. Many fragments of brick which fell into the pit after the removal of the pithos were found in the fill. Later foundations sunk into the pit, and the disturbed earth associated with them, will be discussed in connection with Stratum E.

The two bothroi under A.VI.6, Bothroi 3 and 4, were typical refuse pits. The dark grey fill, which had a greenish tinge in Bothros 3, is the result of the decomposition of quantities of organic matter. Several fragmentary pots were reconstructed from the sherds in Bothros 3. These two bothroi were carefully filled in before the construction of the LC IIIA walls, which lay partly over them.

The two pits under A.V.5, Bothroi 1 and 2, also lay under LC IIIA walls. Bothros 1 was cleared out and filled with stones at the time of the later construction. That the one sherd found in it was of LC II date is probably fortuitous. The upper part of the second pit contained a similar fill, but undisturbed LC II deposit was found at the bottom. Here again dark grey sandy earth indicates organic refuse.

The larger of the two pits under A.V.1, Pit 5, contained dark grey, sandy earth. The small one, Pit 4, was only 0.15 m. deep; it contained three sherds and red brown earth which looked like building debris. Even allowing for some lowering of the level of the bedrock subsequent to the period of these bothroi, the one in question is too shallow to have served any useful purpose as a refuse pit.

The deep cutting between *a.2* and *a.3* was filled in at some time during the LC II period (Benson 1969, 5, A:5; 1970, 25, 40, LC IIA) but presumably later than the time of Stratum A, with *chavara* (crushed sandstone) which contained a minimum of sherds and extraneous matter. Of the few sherds found in this fill, 94% are Neolithic. *Chavara* is commonly dug at present in ancient cemeteries, and the same was probably the case in antiquity. The absence of earth in this fill and the fact that many of the sherds from one part of the fill belong to the same pots as other pieces from other parts of the fill would favor the view that this *chavara* came from a cemetery of the Neolithic period. Distinct Neolithic cemeteries, however, are not yet known in Cyprus, for intramural burial appears to have been customary in that period. Until new evidence appears, it seems more probable that the Bamboula *chavara* came from an eroded region over which there was a thin layer of Neolithic settlement remains. This region has not been found, but it was likely to have been not far from Area A.

Little can be said safely in interpretation of the remains of Stratum A. There is good evidence for walls on cuttings *b* and the eastern part of *a.1*. There is also a strong probability that there were similar walls on foundations *a.2* and *a.3*. Signs of habitation were found in area *c*, but it is not certain whether this area was roofed over or not, nor are its exact dimensions clear. The change in orientation about midway along foundation *a.1* perhaps indicates the dividing point between two houses. Cutting *a.3* presumably belongs to a different house than *a.2*, the space between them serving as a street. One must not overlook the possibility that these were the outer walls of the settlement, and that the narrow passage between *a.2* and *a.3* was part of a gateway. Its narrowness would greatly facilitate its defense. This interpretation is favored by the fact that although many bothroi were found within the area of the cuttings, there was no certain case of one outside this area.

STRATUM B

A number of fragmentary walls of a second building period, of LC IIB (Benson 1969, 5-6, B:1-5; 1970, 41, LC IIB), were found to the north of, and partly overlapping, the remains of Stratum A. Cutting *a.1* is still used, and the difference in levels is so slight that it might appear that these walls belong to Stratum A, were it not that Walls I and II (fig. 3) lie on Stratum A(4) and that Walls III and IV cut Stratum A(3).

The preserved walls appear to belong to two separate buildings, as both Walls I and II, and III and IV appear to form exterior angles. Walls I and II and the enclosed patch of floor are thus assigned to House A.II, the remaining structures to House A.III. A.III appears to have been a residence; A.II may have been a guard-house or some other appendage of the Circuit Wall.

The walls of A.II were built of rubble of fair-sized river stones, unworked and laid without binder. They are preserved to a height of more than 0.35 m. A small fragment of a floor of brown earth was found in the angle of the walls. Over this lay 0.17 m. of what appears to be building debris, the only such debris found *in situ* in Stratum B. The destruction of the levels over this, as of the bulk of A.II, was occasioned by the rebuilding of the Circuit Wall in the Archaic period.

House A.III contained at least four rooms, of which scanty traces have been found under later remains in the area. The largest of these rooms, A.III.1, was 2.70 m. wide by at least 3.65 m. long. No traces of the floor or other remnants from its occupation are preserved. Walls III and IV were cut through Stratum A(3) and founded on the bedrock. Only the foundation trenches and the lowest parts of the foundations are preserved. Of Wall III only the leveling course has survived, but the stones of Wall IV have some order and must come close to the floor level. Wall V is scantily preserved, except under the later northeast wall of A.V.1, where several courses remain. A number of large river stones which were found at the edge of cutting *a.1* may be an extension of Wall VII, and belong to the southwestern wall of Room 1.

The narrow Room 2 was enclosed by Walls V, VI and VII. Wall VII is similar to those already described. Little was preserved save under the later southeastern wall of A.IV.1. The single preserved course of Wall VI consists of sun-dried bricks laid flat on a bedding of beaten earth. The lack of a stone foundation is striking. Two sections of the plaster floor of A.III.2 were cleared, on either side of the northeastern wall of the later A.V.1. This plaster appears to have been a composition of *chavara* and lime; it was a favorite building material in all periods on Bamboula. The floor is on a higher level than the preserved course of Wall VI, but both the floor and the accumula-

tion over it stop in a straight line over the southeastern edge of the wall, showing that this once rose at the side of the floor. Ashy earth containing many sherds was found over the floor, accumulation from the last stage of occupation.

Another narrow room was enclosed by Walls VII and VIII. The floor was not preserved. Wall VIII was in nature and preservation similar to the other stone walls of the period; it was well preserved under A.IV.1, poorly elsewhere.

Room A.III.4 appears to have been a large room comparable with A.III.1; its northwestern and northeastern limits were not determined. It had a floor of hard, very dark red clay, which was found under both Rooms A.IV.1 and A.IV.2 of the following period.

House III collapsed at the end of Stratum B and was in due course succeeded by Stratum C. It is impossible to tell how much time elapsed between the destruction and the rebuilding of the area, but it is clear that the walls of Stratum B were still visible when the later house was built. If this were not so, it would be impossible to explain the fact that the walls of House A.III were well preserved where they lay under the later walls, but almost completely destroyed elsewhere. The only explanation is that the plan of the later building was already determined when the debris of A.III was removed, and that the earlier foundations were left for support wherever later walls were to be built. The other walls were all torn out and the debris was carefully worked over in the search for building stone and usable brick.

In the high region up the hill from cutting *a.1* the debris was cleared off to bedrock, and all the useless material was dumped into a depression below the early cutting, filling it and giving a regular grade to the entire area. This fill went to the preserved walls of House A.II, but no trace of it has been found beyond them, nor in the immediate vicinity of the Circuit Wall. This indicates that House A.II continued to stand after the end of Period B, strengthening the possibility that A.II was part of the defense system; it also increases the probability that the Circuit Wall was erected at the time of Stratum B.

STRATUM C

HOUSE A.IV (pl. 2a-c)
Benson 1969, 6-7

Scanty remains of a third stratum, also of LC IIB date (Benson 1969, 6-7, C:1-3; 1970, 41, LC IIB), were found over those of Stratum B in the northwestern part of the old Trench 2 (fig. 4). There was nothing to indicate that the remainder of the area was inhabited at this time, although it is extremely probable that it was, and that the houses were destroyed in the rebuilding of Period D. House A.IV, which was built at this time over the ruins of A.III, is important in that it remained in use into the following Period D, thus bridging the gap between the LC II and LC III periods. The house apparently collapsed at the end of Period C (Benson 1969, 7, D:1, House IV, Rooms 1 and 3), but was rebuilt on the same foundations in the following period. While it is usually possible to tell, at least in part, which walls were of the original period, it has not been possible to distinguish later rebuilding. The one exception is the wall between A.IV.1 and 2, which was reinforced by a second wall built against it in Period D.

Because of the continued occupation of the house and the unusual tidiness of its occupants, little floor deposit or accumulation of Period C was found. Exceptions, of which the most notable was A.IV.1, will be noted below.

House A.IV was set farther back from the Circuit Wall than its predecessors. This fact, plus the deep fill of Stratum B(5) which was thrown in to prepare for the construction of Stratum C, are arguments in favor of dating the construction of the Circuit Wall to this period. But this question must be reserved for the later discussion of the Circuit Wall; that the wall antedates Period D is certain.

Our best evidence for House A.IV comes from the following Stratum D. Of the four rooms for which we have evidence at that time, three preserved remains of Stratum C as well; presumably all four formed part of the original house. The house projects into the unexcavated area on the northwest; so its full extent is not known.

Room A.IV.1 was long and narrow, terminating in a door which gave into A.IV.3. The northeastern wall of the room was not found, so that there

is a possibility that it was merely a vestibule opening onto the street without an outer gateway. In view, however, of the fact that it had a floor of *chavara* plaster, and that many fragments of vases were found on this floor, it seems more probable that it was an enclosed room. The two long walls lie in footing trenches which cut the deposit of Stratum B, and which are in turn covered by the plaster floor. As noted above, the foundations of the earlier stratum were left intact under the later walls, though destroyed elsewhere.[5]

The northwestern part of the doorway between A.IV.1 and A.IV.3 has been destroyed by an intrusion, so that its exact width cannot be determined. It obviously extended beyond the preserved 0.70 m., though not much, if it followed the usual Bamboula plan of being at a corner rather than at the center of the wall. Good fortune has preserved enough of the step within the doorway to enable us to restore it with a tolerable degree of certainty.

The plaster floor of A.IV.1 terminated in a straight line at the point where the southeastern wall of A.IV.3 joins that of A.IV.1. Beyond this line, toward A.IV.3, is a depression 0.15 m. wide, 0.08 m. below the floor of A.IV.1 and 0.02 m. below that of A.IV.3, where a section of the Stratum C floor is preserved, incorporated into a later pavement. This sinking presumably held a wooden threshold and step, the upper surface of which was flush with the floor in A.IV.1, and which extended to the line where the floor resumes in A.IV.3. The depression of 0.02 m. below the level of the floor in A.IV.3 was sufficient to hold the threshold/step in place. Immediately adjoining this depression, in the eastern corner of A.IV.3, was a small stone with a pivot hole drilled

---

5. An apparent exception is the piece of Wall V of Stratum B, which is preserved under the northeast-eastern wall of A.V.1. This latter wall, however, lies on deposit of both Strata C and D, and thus clearly belongs to Stratum D; it could, therefore, have had no direct connection with the preservation of the wall of Stratum B. Two explanations seem possible, either that there is a wall of Stratum C under the visible wall of the following period, or else that there was such a wall here in Stratum C, but that it was removed prior to the construction of House A.V in the following period. What connection this wall had with House A.IV is not clear.

in the top embedded in the plaster floor. This held the door which opened into A.IV.3 and closed against the face of the wooden threshold.

The earlier wall between A.IV.1 and 2 lay on a regular bed of clay which was placed on the bed-rock save where it ran over the *chavara* fill in the foundation trenches of Walls VII and VIII of Stratum B. This clay bed is well preserved and enables us to trace the course of the wall in spite of the fact that only a small portion of the actual masonry is preserved. A large fragment of LH III ware (B1121) which was built into the stone part of the wall gives a valuable chronological point in the history of the house. This wall was coated with clay during Period D.

All but the southeast walls of A.IV.2, 3 and 4 were destroyed when the house was abandoned at the end of Period D. The position of these walls, however, is determined approximately by the trenches through the Stratum D debris, dug for the purpose of robbing the stones from the walls, as well as by the leveling of the rock to hold the walls. A few stones, including a pivot block, are perhaps *in situ* in the wall between A.IV.3 and 4.

It has already been noted that a piece of the original plaster floor of A.IV.3 was incorporated into the Period D floor of that room and thus was preserved. A patch of clay which adjoins this along the southeastern wall of the room contained LC II sherds and appears to be a repair of the original floor, also of Period C. The sherds found with the large pithos in Pit 1 are all of LC II date and perhaps indicate that this pithos was placed in position during Period C, remaining in use into the subsequent period, when it is clear that it was still visible.

Some ten centimeters of accumulation of Stratum C were found over the plaster floor of A.IV.1. The bulk of the decorated pottery is of LC II types, but much of the plain ware was made on the fast wheel, thus anticipating the following LC IIIA period. Two decorated sherds of LC IIIA type may easily be intrusive, though there are reasons to believe that this ware was coming into use in the latter part of the LC II period.

A fair depth of earth accumulated over the deep fill of Stratum B(5) during the course of Period C in the region between House A.IV and the Circuit Wall. No trace of house walls was found in this level.

STRATUM D

The beginning of the LC III period was marked by great building activity on Bamboula, the last such period in the history of the site. In view of the gradual abandonment of the site beginning at the end of the LC IIIA period, the remains of this stratum are relatively well preserved. The thoroughness with which the ground was pre-pared for the construction of the buildings of Stratum D, on the other hand, caused the destruc-tion of many of the remains of earlier date. As a result of these two factors, the LC IIIA period is much the most fully represented of any in the Bamboula settlement.

On most parts of Bamboula we found only one main building level of the LC III period; numer-ous repairs show that the period must have lasted a relatively long time. In the main part of Area A, however, four distinct building levels of LC III were isolated, in Strata D, E, F and G. Both Strata D and E were substantial, though a slight decrease in the occupied area was noted in Stratum E. Strata F and G, on the other hand, are limited to

a small area and clearly belonged to a time when the settlement on Bamboula had ceased to func-tion as an important urban agglomeration. Apart, however, from the the main section of Area A and a few of the tombs, remains contemporary with Stratum E were not found elsewhere on the site, so that we must conclude that Bamboula was rapidly losing its importance even at this time. Reasons will be shown below[6] for dividing the LC III period into two sub-phases; LC IIIA corre-sponds with Stratum D in Area A and the single LC III stratum of other parts of the site; LC IIIB is represented by Strata E-G in Area A.

Extensive clearing and quarrying was under-taken prior to the construction of the houses of Stratum D. With the exception of A.IV, which remained in use from the previous period, and the deep LC II fill below the cutting of Stratum A, all that part of Area A which was inhabited in Period D was cleared to bedrock. Only the both-

---

6. See also Daniel 1938, 267-69.

roi of the earlier periods escaped. When the plans of the new houses were determined, the bedrock was cut out still more in many places to supply regular and fairly level floors. The rock was usually not cut where the walls were to be, so that there are in many cases tall ridges of living rock under the walls. It is, of course, possible that the walls were built before the floors were finished between them, but whatever the exact chronological sequence, it is clear that the two operations were intimately connected.

At least four houses and part of a fifth were cleared in Stratum D of Area A. These appear to have been the dwellings of ordinary citizens. There is nothing palatial about them, and yet they have the appearance of a good, solid economy. Five or six rooms seem to have been about standard. The walls were built of sun-dried brick laid over foundations of stone rubble; the stones were unhewn save occasionally at corners and by doorways. The masonry appears to have been covered with clay. There is some slight evidence that the roofs closely resembled those of the present-day village houses, having a slight slope to one side and being covered with clay (*konnos*) borne on a bedding of straw or matting over transverse beams. The rooms approach, but never quite attain, rectangularity. Most of the floors were of smoothed bedrock or *chavara* plaster. The doorways were at or near the corners of the rooms. Some had well-built stone or wooden jambs and thresholds; pivot blocks indicate at least a limited use of swinging doors.

THE STREET

The houses were set well back from the Circuit Wall and the intervening area was left open to serve as a street and to facilitate defense. The section nearest to the houses was coated with lime and packed by many feet; this was doubtless the street proper. The doors of nearby houses opened on to it. During the course of the period, regulations appear to have been relaxed, for the owners of the houses fenced off sections of the street and appropriated them for private use. One such fence crossed the street close to the junction of Houses A.V. and VI. Here were found two deep post holes containing carbonized wood, and with stones around the sides to hold the posts in place. A ridge of earth connected the two post holes, as

earth usually collects along a fence. Shallow trenches and a row of stones, which may have carried a garden wall, were found northeast of House A.IV. The earth between this row of stones and the house was packed and strewn with broken pottery, proof that this too was taken over for private purposes; it does not appear ever to have formed part of the house proper.

The street and the area between it and the Circuit Wall remained in use for the duration of Stratum E. During this time the street was often resurfaced, and the level rose accordingly (Benson 1969, 8, D:2).

HOUSE A.IV (pl. 2a–c)
Benson 1969, 7–8, 11

The prior history of House A.IV (fig. 4) has been discussed in connection with Stratum C. So far as our evidence goes, the plan of the house was, with one exception, the same in Stratum D as in C. At the beginning of Period D a poorly constructed stone wall, 0.40 m. wide, was built against the southeast side of the wall between A.IV.1 and 2, to give additional support. Whereas in the rest of the house all deposit of Stratum C was cleared out to bedrock or solid floors, in A.IV.1 the early accumulation was left, and the reinforcement of the wall rests on this level. This suggests that the wall was reinforced before the debris was cleared out of the rest of the house and implies that the original wall was still standing, though in precarious condition, at the time that the rebuilding was undertaken.

The top of the Stratum C accumulation in A.IV.1 was used as floor in Stratum D, without any special surfacing. Very little earth accumulated over this floor during Period D, and the debris of the walls lay just a few centimeters over the Stratum C level. Whatever the use of A.IV.1 in Period C, it appears improbable that it was one of the main living rooms of the house during Period D.

A.IV.2 remained unchanged in Period D, save that the walls were coated with clay. All debris of the preceding period was removed, and the bedrock served as floor throughout Period D. A belly-amphora (B915) was standing on the floor when the house collapsed; its fragments were found lying under the fallen walls of the house.

Part of the Stratum C floor of A.IV.3 was re-used in Stratum D. The floor in this period consisted in part of the earlier floor, in part of bedrock, in part of *chavara* fill lying over Stratum A(6), and in part of patches of earth thrown in to fill up small holes. The entire floor was covered with lime, which must have given it a more unified appearance. Some 0.04 m. of closely stratified successive floorings lay over this first floor of Stratum D. A cylindrical stone lies in approximately the center of the room on the accumulation (pl. 2b). This is a post support placed there late in the history of the house to give added support to a weakened roof. An oval-shaped depression, with inner measurements of 0.155 m. by 0.165 m., on the upper surface of the support indicates the dimensions of the wooden post which stood on it. A large pithos (B932) was found in fragments in Pit 1, near the southwest wall of the room (pl. 2b). It was sunk from the original floor, probably during Period C (see above pp. 8-9), but remained in use until the final destruction of the house. The fragments of a plain, hand-made jug were found with it and presumably belong to the latest use of the pithos, in Period D. Three pots of plain ware (B852, 815, 916) and a clay lamp (B1575) were found in fragments on the accumulation, broken when the house collapsed. More than 0.30 m. of building debris were found in this room.

The floor of A.IV.4 consisted of bedrock in the northwest and of *chavara* fill over Stratum A(6) in the southeast. The *chavara* of the fill was so pure that it was not noted that it was fill rather than bedrock while it was being excavated. The difference was first observed as the floor dried out; the fill dried more rapidly and was thereby isolated. There was no direct proof that A.IV.4 was used in the time of Stratum C, but since the rest of the house goes back to that time, it is altogether probable that this room does too.

Three pits were sunk into the floor of A.IV.4 to hold storage jars (pl. 2c). Two of these jars, a pithos (B931) and an amphoroid krater (B946), were found *in situ*; the third, a shoulder amphora with inscribed rim (B942), was found lying in pieces on accumulation 0.05 m. over the original floor. Apparently an attempt was made to remove it when the collapse of the house seemed imminent, but it broke while being carried out of the

room and was left lying where it fell. Two decorated bowls (B553, 409) were found in the accumulation, and a number of stone objects on it. The latter comprise six rubbers (B1482), three pestles (B1492) and a whetstone. In the northwestern edge of the excavated area a limestone basin can be seen lying on the accumulation. It appears to resemble that found on the northeast corner of the foundation between A.V. and A.VI of Stratum F. Some 0.40 m. of building tumble lay over the accumulation in this room.

House IV was not rebuilt after its collapse at the end of Period D. The space over the ruins of the house remained open, and the level of the ground was gradually raised by silt and miscellaneous accumulation. Soon after the collapse of the house, the debris was gone over for usable building material. All sizable stones and whole bricks were removed for use elsewhere, perhaps in House A.VIII, which was built in Period E. It may even be that A.VIII was built by the former owners of A.IV, who preferred its higher and drier position. That this salvaging took place immediately after the end of Period D is proven by the fact that the trenches sunk to remove the stones were not found above the debris of Stratum D, that the debris included no potsherds later than Period D, and that walls which were needed in Period E were not molested. These walls are the party wall with House A.V, which was rebuilt in Period E, and the reinforcement of the northwest wall of A.IV.1, which was probably kept to form a shed for A.V. A few stones of the original northwest wall of A.IV.1 escaped by chance; otherwise hardly a stone remained of House A.IV, either *in situ* or in the fallen debris.

HOUSE A.V (pl. 2d)
Benson 1969, 7, 9, 11; 1970, 25

House A.V, built in LC IIIA, is an excellent example of a type of house common in the later levels of Bamboula (fig. 5). Though the type is capable of more or less elaboration, the known examples all present certain fixed features. The house plan is an L, each arm of which is composed of two or more rooms. With the possible exception of House A.VIII, another room or series of rooms occupies the angle between the two arms of the L; one of its exterior walls is flush with the end wall of one arm of the L, but the other exterior wall falls somewhat short of the end wall of the other arm of the L. The corner room, common to both arms of the L, is usually as wide as one of the arms of the L, less wide than the other, leaving space for communication between the two wings of the house without passing through the corner room. There is an exterior, unroofed, courtyard associated with each such house. The rooms are connected with doorways both into the corner room and directly into the adjoining room of the other wing of the house. There is no available evidence that the corner room was directly accessible from outdoors.

House A.V represents this basic plan reduced to its simplest form: one wing consists of Rooms 1 and 2, the other of Rooms 3 and 4. Room 2 is the corner room connecting the two wings. The space between the two wings is occupied by Room 5; its northwest wall is almost flush with that of Room 1 and forms a party wall with House A.IV. The southwest wall of A.V.5 lies 0.90 m. short of that of Room 4. The area southwest of A.V was open during Period D; the area adjacent to Room 5 was specially adapted to household purposes and remained open even after House A.VIII was built in Period E.

The wall between A.V.1 and 2 is diagonal, giving the two rooms the shape of parallelograms. Evidence will be presented below to show that there was a doorway at the southwestern end of this wall, near the large slab on the floor of Room 2. Two northwest walls are preserved in Room 1. Only the outer one is of Stratum D; the other was added in the following period for extra support. House A.V was entered from the street through Room 1. The doorway has a minimum width of 1.00 m. No trace of a threshold or jambs was found, and the irregular opening might seem to preclude the possibility that it was ever closed by a door; yet a door opening inward would be perfectly feasible, and in all probability existed.

Room 3 had no less than four doorways, giving direct access to each room of the house. Nothing remains of the fittings of the doorway to Room 1. A few stones suggest a raised threshold in the doorway to Room 2, though these may simply be the remnants of filling in the door subsequent to Period D. The doorways into Rooms 4 and 5 were filled in at a later date, but their original and subsequent arrangements are clear, perhaps more so

than any place else on Bamboula. The doorway to Room 4 is 0.60 m. wide. The southeast jamb consists of a regular, but apparently unhewn, rectangular block of limestone standing on end 0.15 m. back of the base of the wall. No jamb or pivot block has been found at the northwestern side of the doorway; the door presumably shut against the southwestern jamb. A combined threshold and step up into Room 4 consists of a row of river stones some 0.10 m. above the level of the floor.

The doorway into Room 5 is 0.90 m. wide and used the bedrock for a threshold. A small stone with a pivot hole in its upper surface was embedded in the floor of Room 5 close by the northeast side of the door, showing that the door swung from this side and into Room 5 (pl. 2d). The threshold was raised at the beginning of Period E, and the preserved part of the doorway was walled up at a later date. Neither the higher threshold nor the rubble filling extends to the southwestern limit of the opening, but the last 0.15 m. are filled with relatively clean earth. It is obvious that something which is no longer preserved occupied the western end of the doorway when the later remodelings took place, and that the earth which now stands in this position came in as the missing object decayed following the collapse of the house. This can only have been a wooden jamb, traces of which may still remain in the undug fill of the doorway. The doorway leading from A.V.5 into the outdoor courtyard was about 0.50 m. wide. Nothing of its fittings remains.

Pits of various size and for various purposes were common on Bamboula, but never so much so as in the LC IIIA period. A nest of four small pits, 2-5, lay along the northwest wall of A.V.2. Pits 2-3 were covered by a flat limestone slab 0.40 by 1.10 m. Pit 1 of Stratum E grazed the slab and cut into Pit 2. Pits 4-5 were not covered and were empty at the end of Period D. Pits 2-3 contained fragments of two vases (B913, 855), the other fragments of which were found lying on the accumulation over the floor of the room, directly under the wall tumble of the end of Period D. The fragments in the pits must have gotten there at the very end of Period D, and this would have been possible only if the slab covering them were lifted. We have seen already that houses of this type usually had a doorway connecting the two rooms of a wing. The northeast part of the wall between Rooms 1 and 2 is preserved and had no such opening; the southwest part of the wall is destroyed, so that there is no direct evidence. The presence of a slab used to cover the pits directly in front of the place where such a doorway would have been is strong evidence in favor of the existence of such a doorway. The slab was left in position except when access to the pits was desired; it was then lifted and replaced again so as not to impede passage through the doorway.

A pithos (B930) was sunk in the large Pit 1 near the center of A.V.3. The lip of the pithos was broken; so a sherd from a similar vase was placed outside the break and held in position by packing it with earth. A jug (B848) stood in a small pit, 2, against the northeast wall. This pit cut a smaller pit, which was faced with plaster. A shallow pit, 3, in the western corner of the room contained fragments of two painted bowls (B425, 492). A tall platform of brick rubble coated with a thick layer of clay stood in the southern corner of the room; this remained in use into Period E.

There were three pits in A.V.4: Pit 1 contained fragments of a painted bowl (B440); this pit was open at the end of Period D, for the building debris went into it. Pit 2 was filled up prior to the end of Period D. In its sandy fill were found a bronze chisel (B1303) and awl (B1305). A shallow pit in the western corner contained nothing of interest.

Earth accumulated over all the floors during the course of Period D and was trod in thin horizontal strata. In Room 5 it was not possible to distinguish between accumulation of Strata D and E.

The house walls on Bamboula were not usually bonded together, but were built in segments abutting each other. This makes chronological conclusions from the junctions of walls difficult. It can be stated, however, that House A.V was built subsequent to House A.VI, for whereas all the cross walls of House V abut on the party wall with House VI, this party wall is bonded into the southwest wall of House VI. There is, however, absolutely no reason to think that the chronological priority of House VI was considerable; the difference may be one of only a very short time.

Little building debris of Period D was found in House A.V, and yet it is clear that it collapsed. As in most of the houses on Bamboula, the debris was largely removed prior to rebuilding. Only 0.09 m. of debris were found in Room 4; yet evidence will be presented below to show that at least the southwest wall of the room had to be rebuilt for Period E. No tumble of Period D was found in either Room 1 or 5, but part of the party wall between Rooms 1 and 2 was found lying in order on the floor of Room 2, and the same was true of the wall between Rooms 3 and 5, remains of which were found in Room 3. Since at least one wall of each room collapsed at the end of Period D, there is no doubt that the house was destroyed at that time.

HOUSE A.VI (pl. 3a-c)
Benson 1969, 8-9, 11

House A.VI, also of LC IIIA date, has a plan which, as reconstructed, is unique in Area A, but occurs also in Area E. The reconstruction has a fair degree of probability in spite of the fact that this region suffered greatly from operations incidental to the rebuilding of the Circuit Wall in the Archaic period. As noted above (p. 7), a large area was dug out back of the wall at that time. This excavation did a great deal of damage to the eastern part of House A.VI. The walls which appear on fig. 6 in broken lines were completely destroyed; the excavation in the Archaic period was carried to bedrock in this section. West of this area that excavation became progressively shallower, disappearing entirely in the northeast third of A.VIII.1 (see fig. 24). In A.VIII.1, Strata F and G and the building debris of Stratum E were destroyed in the northeast part of the room; the highest level left in A.VIII.2 is Stratum E, and only a small bit of it survives. The disturbance came low over the western part of A.VI.4 and went to bedrock throughout the east. The east-central part of A.VI.5 is disturbed to the rock, but undisturbed deposit of Strata D and E was found in the northeast, as well as in the northwest part of A.VI.2. The very eastern corner of A.VI.3 was also disturbed.

The position of the southeast, northeast and northwest walls of A.VI.4 is assured by the beveling at the edge of the preserved plaster floor (pl. 3a). The northeast end of the northwest wall and the northeast wall of the room are indicated by stone foundations built into the large LC II pit in the northern corner of the room (pl. 3a). The preserved foundations in this place are of Period E, but there is no reasonable doubt that they replace earlier foundations in the same place. The northeast wall of the house is partly preserved in A.VI.3, and the bed on which it lay can be traced in most of A.VI.2. The restoration of A.VI.1 is conjectural, though highly probable in view of what is preserved elsewhere. All other walls are fairly well preserved.

The house consists of three long units, each of which is composed of a long and a short room, connected by a door at one corner. The three long rooms—4, 5 and 6—were apparently connected by other doors. There is no evidence that the short rooms could be entered directly from one another. The broad doorway between Rooms 2 and 5 suggests that the main entrance to the house was through Room 2, from the street. The preservation of the northeast wall of Room 2 does not permit the determining of the position or nature of this door. No trace of a threshold, jamb or pivot was found in the doorway between Rooms 2 and 5. This, in combination with its width of 1.50 m., suggests that it was never closed by a door. The doorway between Rooms 5 and 6 is 1.20 m. wide, flanked on its southwest side by large and fairly regular blocks which run the full width of the wall. Here, too, no fittings for a door were found, but investigation was not carried out under the threshold of Stratum E. The doorway between Rooms 6 and 3 is only 0.50 m. wide; here too fittings for a door are missing, though this may be because of a recent intrusion which reached bedrock here. This doorway gives on to a platform in Room 3, consisting of a core of earth held in place by mud bricks placed on edge. Two stones are wedged between the brick and the northwest wall of the room. The platform rises 0.33 m. above the floor of Room 3, and is nearly flush with the floor of Room 6. The bricks measure about 0.63 by 0.33 by 0.12 m.

The floors of Rooms 4 and 5 consisted of *chavara* plaster, well laid and beveled up to the walls. The other rooms used the bedrock as floor, save northeast of the cutting of Period A, where earlier deposit was used. A limestone slab was placed over the LC II bothros which runs partly under the northwest wall of Room 6. Flat stones embedded in the floor of Rooms 3 and 5 seem to have served as supports for roof posts.

A low rectangular compartment with plaster walls was built against the southwest wall of Room 4 (pl. 3b); its exact purpose is not certain, though it probably served in preparation of food. A small pot was embedded in the pavement slightly east of the center of the same room. The broken bottom of a jug was similarly embedded in the floor of Room 5, close to the doorway into 6. An inscribed storage amphora (B941) stood in the pit at the northeast end of Room 6 (pl. 3c). The vase was standing intact covered with a limestone lid when the house collapsed. The weight of the debris broke it, and the fragments were found lying in order in the pit, under 0.25 m. of tumble. Three other pots (B700, 926, 934) were found on the accumulation in Room 6, while a bowl (B497) lay on accumulation in Room 3.

Shallow deposits of earth which accumulated during the course of Period D were found in Rooms 3, 4 and 6. The floor of Room 5 was kept clean until the house collapsed. In Room 2 there was 0.28 m. of loose burned deposit containing many fragments of vases (B408, 439). This does not look like ordinary accumulation, but may well be the debris from an upper storey.

Large patches of soft white clay without any potsherds or other extraneous matter lay over the floor of Room 5. Some was found in the pot embedded in the floor, directly under the usual building debris; there were also some patches over the fill above the LC II well. Its patchy nature, its purity and its softness show that it was not paving and never had been trod on. It lay on the floor and was immediately covered by the usual wall debris. This was, no doubt, *konnos* used as roofing material. A thick coating placed over reeds or matting stretched across the rafters makes a roof that is waterproof for a number of years and is easily renewed. There has been little change in Cypriote architectural technique through the centuries, and it seems likely that the clay found in Room 5 is roofing material. If so, it means that the roof fell first, reaching the floor before the walls collapsed on top of it. If this is the case, the fact that the roof material lay directly on the floor indicates that there was no second storey over Room 5. Similar roofing material was found directly over the Stratum E floor in A.VI.4.

Fallen wall debris to a depth varying from 0.07 m. to 0.25 m. was found in House A.VI. As in the case of the other houses, it is clear that much of the debris was cleared out before rebuilding in the following period.

HOUSE A.VIa (pl. 3d)
Benson 1969, 8-9, 11

It is possible to give only an incomplete report on this house, still of LC IIIA date, of which only parts of three rooms were excavated and walls apparently belonging to it were found under the later walls of A.VIII[7] (fig. 7). Of the three rooms mentioned above, Room 3 was only partly excavated, Room 1 was largely cleared out when House A.VIII was built in the following period, and all three rooms were badly damaged by the Archaic period excavations for the Circuit Wall. The house of Stratum D to which these rooms belong shared a party wall with House A.VI, but most of the house lay under A.VIII of Stratum E (see fig. 24). House A.VIa was abandoned at the end of Period D.

The foundations of the southwest walls of the house are fairly well preserved in A.VIa.2, less well in Room 1, and better again in the stretch of wall just inside of the southwest walls of A.VIII.3 and 4. Those of Rooms 1 and 2 lie in foundation trenches which cut earlier fill and bedrock. The line of the wall between Rooms 2 and 3 is easily traced by the rock shelf on which the wall stood and by a few fragments of masonry; it was the continuation of the southwest wall of House A.VI. Under the southwest walls of A.VIII.3 and 4, of Stratum E, lay an earlier wall which formed part of A.VIa. The northwest wall of A.VIII.4 lay in a deep foundation trench. Two large round holes sunk below this foundation trench, at about the middle of the side towards A.VIII.4, look like post holes. Both foundation trench and post holes probably belonged to A.VIa.

Since these walls of House A.VIII.3 and 4 so closely follow the lines of earlier walls of A.VIa, it is logical to expect that the wall between A.VIII. 3 and 4 also reflects an earlier wall; otherwise the room in House A.VIa would be exceptionally large. We would, therefore, suggest a reconstruc-

tion of House A.VIa with two similar rooms, 4 and 5, but this remains conjectural for lack of evidence of this wall.

The floor of Room 2 is of packed sandy clay, lying over some 0.30 m. of earlier fill. In the west, where the disturbance of the Archaic period did little damage, 0.37 m. of fallen debris lay over the floor. The floor of Room 1 also lay on earlier fill. This floor was destroyed when House A.VIII was built, but some of the fill beneath it was recovered. A door in the north corner of Room 2 had a paving of plaster laid over the leveling course of the wall.

The floor of Room 3 is well preserved; it consists of packed grey brown earth on which lie four large and several smaller stone slabs (pl. 3d). The upper surface of one of these slabs bears three rows of shallow holes, perhaps cut with a metal tool. This device was commonly in use in later times to prevent slipping in wet weather and probably explains this piece. It is improbable, however, that this stone is in its original position; it appears to have been salvaged from an earlier threshold. Some 0.06 m. of accumulation lay over this floor, and 0.25 m. of tumble over this. The tumble was once deeper than this, but was cut into by the disturbance of the Archaic period.

The plan of House A.VIa remains enigmatic because it is so incompletely known. The position of Room 3 suggests that the house may originally have had more rooms that were destroyed when House A.VI was built, implying that A.VIa antedated A.VI. The house would then most likely have been of the typical L-shaped plan. What has been reconstructed from known remains forms an L-shaped plan, including Rooms 1, 2, 4 and 5, but room 3 is aberrant.

HOUSE A.VII (pl. 4a-c)
Benson 1969, 9-11

Under this heading are included all the house remains uncovered in the northwestern part of Area A, a section originally labeled Trench 4 (fig. 8). It is not at all certain that all the remains found here belong to one house, but since no satisfactory means of differentiation has been found, it seems advisable to consider them as a unit. All seem to date originally to LC IIIA.

This section is connected with the main part of Area A by a trench 9.50 m. long and 1.50 m. wide

---

7. While Daniel had realized that the house was larger than just the three rooms, A.VIa.1-3, he did not have time to investigate it further. I was able to do only a small amount of work in 1951, but it indicated the further extension of the house.

(Trench 10, fig. 24). The excavation of this trench was not carried to the floor levels, but sufficed to show the orientation and location of some walls. The remains in this trench probably belong to a house of Stratum D, but apparently not to any of those houses cleared.

House A.VII has suffered considerable disturbance. The western part of the house lies so close to the surface that bedrock is scarred by the plow in several places. In the better preserved part of Room 3 and in Room 8 the disturbance reached to within a few centimeters of the floor. Even those parts of the trench which were not reached by the plow have suffered greatly from the exploratory pits of treasure hunters. The would-be plunderers, in their enthusiasm, often dug deep into the bedrock below the house floors. As a result of this, several points relating to the house plan and stratification remain obscure. Crucial parts of many walls are destroyed, so that only four doorways can be located; this is a serious handicap in attempting to decide whether the rooms preserved belong to one or several houses.

The rebuilding of one wall and the closing of several doorways indicate that there was a second period of habitation and a reconstructed house over the level of the preserved deposit. Unfortunately, we found no deposit which can be assigned to this second stratum. The preserved remains appear on ceramic evidence to be contemporary with those of Stratum D in the remainder of Area A. The reoccupation here probably corresponded with Stratum E.[8]

The rooms of House A.VII, which are approximately rectangular, are knit together in a highly confused manner. The floor plan does not resemble that of any other house found on Bamboula, although in the unit formed by Rooms 4 to 10 there is a resemblance to the L-shaped plan.

The wall at the northwest end of Room 10 is of double thickness. This is all original construction, not to be confused with the secondary reinforcements observed elsewhere. Rooms 9, 10 and 11 are at a much lower level than the rest of the house; this considered in conjunction with the thick walls indicates that there was a second storey

over at least Room 10, but probably over all three.

Room 6 contained the foundations of a stairway which led to the upper storey. The room is enclosed by rubble walls on three sides, possibly on the fourth as well, though a recent intrusion has destroyed the southwest wall. Another intrusion disturbed the interior of the room to somewhat below the preserved tops of the walls; the lower, undisturbed, deposit within the room consists of a great mass of stones. These have been removed only partly, but it is already clear that they go well below the predominant floor level of this section, so that it is unlikely that they are wall debris. These stones appear to have been placed here intentionally, perhaps as a foundation for a stairway. Such a stairway could have started in Room 4 and led up to the second storey over Room 9.

Five doorways can be established with relative certainty: one of these led from Room 2 into Room 4. It was 1.00 m. wide and was fitted with a threshold of large, flat stones. When the house was rebuilt, after its collapse at the end of Period D, a new threshold, again of large flat blocks, was established at a higher level. In the second period of House A.VII, presumably our Period E, a doorway led from the west corner of Room 7 into Room 3. The wall through which this doorway opens replaced an earlier wall in almost the same position. While we have no proof, it may well be that there was a doorway in approximately this same position in Period D. A third doorway connected Room 9 with the southern corner of Room 11 in Stratum D; it was 0.50 m. wide. This doorway was walled up in a sloppy manner in the following period. The fourth door lay at the northern end of the wall between Rooms 8 and 12; it too was walled up in the following period. This doorway was about 0.70 m. wide and was faced with rough-hewn rectangular blocks. The northern face has been dislocated by an intrusion, but the lower course remains, only slightly out of place. Two well-shaped blocks which probably formed part of the doorway were found in the disturbed earth of the intrusion. Another type of doorway, actually the opening between two corners formed by walls, connects Rooms 5 and 7; it is only ca. 0.50 m. wide.

No other doorways could be identified, though

---

8. See Benson 1969, 10, who thinks this may be debris from the second storey, rather than reoccupation.

others must have existed at one time. There was probably no means of direct access between Rooms 9, 10 and 11 and the higher rooms to the southwest. The difference in level was such that steps would have been necessary, but none were found, although the deep deposit in Rooms 9 and 10 was essentially undisturbed. These rooms may have been entered by a wooden stairway from the second floor or, more probably, through Room 12.

The walls of Stratum D in A.VII were all founded on bedrock. The southwest wall of Room 10 and the southwest and southeast walls of Room 9 lay on raised steps in the rock. The rock crumbled and the walls are poorly preserved. Nothing remains of the masonry of the southwest wall of Room 8, but its location is fixed by the rock step on which it stood, and which is preserved in the southern part of the room. The northwest wall of the room can be placed approximately by a foundation of rough rubble built into the pit by the entrance into Room 12. With the wall in this position, the doorway into Room 12 stood at the corner of the room, the arrangement which appears to have been canonical at this time. The southeastern and southwestern walls of Room 2 are outlined by the edge of the plaster floor which ran to them. The northeastern wall of Room 11 is possibly indicated by a cutting through the undisturbed earth below the floor level of this room. It is, however, quite irregular and does not inspire confidence.

Subsidiary roof supports were found in several rooms: a heavy support of rubble masonry lying on an intermediate level in accumulation in the middle of Room 12, a large stone placed on edge in Room 3, and a stone post with a socket in its upper surface against the northeast wall of Room 8.

An interesting structural complex was found in Room 1, consisting of an oven and a rectangular shaft carefully built of rough-hewn stones (pl. 4a), which came flush with the floor on its east side and rose 0.25 m. above the floor on the west. The floor of the shaft, flat and paved with stones, lay 0.85 m. below the floor of Room 1. The shaft had interior measurements of 0.70 m. by 0.80 m. The oven was built of clay, baked hard by the fire within. It was in the shape of a circle with one side cut off in the line of the northwest wall of the stone-lined pit. Its inner dimensions were 1.00 m. from northeast to southwest by 1.25 m. from southeast to northwest. A horizontal strip of baked clay attached to the top of the northwestern side of the stone-faced pit projects slightly into the area of the oven proper. This seems to be the remnant of a shelf inside the oven. Nothing can be said of the superstructure or purpose of the oven. In spite of the large number of fragments of baked clay found, none casts any light on the shape, and none could be attributed to a door, vent holes or blowpipes. That considerable heat was generated is shown by the fact that many of the stones on the near side of the pit were calcined.

In keeping with the size and apparent importance of this house, many of the floors were hard-surfaced. The smoothed bedrock served as floor in Rooms 3 and 9. Plaster floors were found in Rooms 2, 7, 8, 10 and 11. Floors of earth mixed with lime or *chavara* were found in Rooms 1, 4, 5 and 12. Of these, Room 4 was little more than a passageway, possibly with the beginning of the staircase, Room 5 was a workroom and Room 1 an outside courtyard. A fireplace stood in the south corner of Room 12, which may have been the kitchen of the house. The plaster floors all rest in part on bedrock, in part on fill. The earth floors all lie on fill. There was no such elaborate quarrying here as in the main part of Area A. A covered drain cut into the floor of Room 10 at its southeastern end (pl. 4b).

Several pits were sunk below the floors. Deep bothroi in rooms 3 and 12 were used for general refuse. After being filled up, they were sealed, that in Room 3 with *chavara,* that in Room 12 with clay. Among the contents of the bothros in Room 3 were a bronze needle (B1274), a fragment of an alabaster vase (B1244) and two stone rubbers (B1466, 1467). The large rectangular pit in the north corner of Room 8 was built to hold a pithos. The sides were packed with clay and stones to hold the vessel in place. At some time well before the end of Period D, the pot was broken and the pit was filled. We found many fragments of the pithos, but they were badly rotted and could not be mended. At a later date in Period D, a small pit was dug into the southern part of the fill in the big pit. Four vases (B405, 526, 551, 573) and a stamp seal (B1640) were found in this. A shallow pit in the northern corner of Room 10 contained some fragments of a pithos.

In Rooms 3, 5 and 10 we found a deposit of 0.10 to 0.14 m. of untrodden earth relatively free of stones lying over the highest occupation level but below the wall debris. A considerable amount of pottery and other objects was found on and in this earth. The deposit went down among the objects which were standing on the floors, but did not cover them entirely; it is thus inconceivable that it was a habitation level. The most plausible explanation is that this is debris of a second storey and that the objects found in and on this deposit were on the second floor when the house collapsed.

Important deposits of pottery and other objects which were in use when the house collapsed were found on the floors of House A.VII. On accumulation over the floor of Room 8 were found two pots (B404, 846), a cylinder seal (B1630), a whetstone (B1546) and a saddle quern (B1497). The objects found in the pit have been mentioned above. The fragments of a jug (B876) and a rubber were found on the floor of Room 3. A loom-weight (B1592) and four vases (B847, 865, 1004, 1574) were found in the earth which appears to have fallen from the second floor. Objects in the bothros were mentioned above. Two saddle querns and a fragment of bronze were found in accumulation in Room 12. A shoulder amphora (B940) was sunk in a pit in the floor of room 5 (pl. 4c); its neck projected slightly above the floor and was encircled by a collar of *chavara*. A large and crudely worked stone basin stood at the southern corner of the room. Next to it was a vat (B965), left standing upside down, probably to dry out after use. Debris presumably fallen from the second floor contained a jug (B602), a stone pithos cover (B1494), a stone rubber (B1479) and two saddle querns (B1498, 1499). Another vat (B963) stood on the floor of Room

10. With it were the fragments of a pithos (B933) and a pithos neck (B929) placed on end on the floor. The head of a terracotta rhyton (B1568) was also found on the floor, as were four querns (B1500, 1501), a stone rubber and two stone pithos lids. The cellar-like Room 9 contained a pithos (B926), a bucchero jug (B697) and a pithos neck (B928). On the accumulation in Room 11 were found the fragments of a painted krater (B569), a plain jug (B872), a cooking pot (B975) and two domed seals (B1633, 1634). A jug of plain ware was sunk into the floor of Room 1, just north of the stone-lined shaft. Some fragments of an iron implement were found on the floor of Room 12.

Most of the rooms contained a shallow deposit of earth which accumulated gradually over the floors during the use of the building. The debris from the upper storey which was found in some rooms has been mentioned already. Ordinary debris from the fallen walls lay over this. In the shallow western part of the trench, the original depth of the debris is not known, but in the east it is better preserved than is usually the case at Bamboula. Some 0.40 m. of debris were found over Room 10, 0.62 m. over Room 11 and 0.87 m. over Room 9.

It has been noted in passing that there was some evidence for a second structural period in House A.VII, and it has been suggested that this may possibly, but not necessarily, correspond with Stratum E of the rest of the area. This evidence consists of the walling up of the three known doorways of Stratum D and the rebuilding of the southwestern wall of Room 7. The preserved wall lies on deposit over the Stratum D floor and some 0.10 m. to the east of the edge of the original plaster floor. There are no floors on other deposit which could be assigned to this rebuilding; it appears that all traces of it have been washed away.

STRATUM E

Stratum E is marked by the abandoning of Houses A.IV and A.VIa, the rebuilding of Houses A.V and A.VI, and the construction of House A.VIII.

The most interesting aspect of Stratum E is the appearance of the Proto-White Painted pottery of the LC IIIB period, similar to that found in

Tombs 25 and 26a of the Kaloriziki necropolis, to the south of Bamboula in the coastal plain.[9] This Proto-White Painted style, with roots in the so-called Granary Class pottery of mainland Greece, is generically later than the painted wares

9. Benson 1973, 32-36.

predominant in Stratum D. Daniel saw good reason to think that the introduction of the new style of pottery coincided with the influx of considerable numbers of Achaeans from Greece. His description of the manner in which this pottery appeared at Bamboula is quoted at length in Benson 1970, 39.

THE STREET
Benson 1969, 12, 14

The street remained in use from Period D. The silting up and resurfacing of the road continued without a break, and if the road was blocked temporarily, by a collapse of houses at the end of Period D, nothing remains to show for it. During the course of Period E, the level of the road rose some 0.06 to 0.10 m.; the area between the street and the Circuit Wall rose between 0.08 and 0.20 m. The fence continued to divide the street between Houses A.V and A.VI.

At the end of Period E, the northeast walls of Houses A.V and A.VI fell out into the street and were not cleared off. The debris over the street east of House A.V consists almost entirely of sun-dried brick; that by House A.VI contains a considerable amount of stone in addition to brick. The line of demarcation between the two types of debris coincides with the boundary between the two houses. It might be argued that the two types of debris differ fundamentally and that this favors the assumption of a chronological difference between the two. The preserved foundations of the two houses, however, show that the difference is not chronological. Almost nothing is preserved of the stone foundation of the northeast wall of House A.VI. What little there is shows that it was poorly built upon a thin fill covering the loose, stony fill of Stratum B(5). The stones found in the debris of House A.VI thus come from the foundation, which collapsed along with the rest of the wall. The foundations of the northeast walls of House A.V, on the other hand, were well built of large stones and are preserved in place. These walls lie in part on the remains of house walls of Stratum B, in part on a firm deposit of Strata D(1), C(4) and B(5). In Period F a large stone basin was laid across the adjoining foundations of Houses A.V and A.VI by the street, confirming evidence cited above for the collapse of both houses at the end of Period E.

Despite the fact that the street was frequently resurfaced, there is no difference in the final paving to indicate a time gap between the collapse of the two houses in question. Strict contemporaneity is proved by two sherds of Proto-White Painted ware (B652, 653). Although these are from one and the same vase, one sherd was found on the surface of the street under the debris of House A.V and the other on the same level but under the debris of House A.VI. It must be concluded from this that Houses A.V and A.VI collapsed at the same time, and that this was after the introduction of Proto-White Painted ware.

HOUSE A.V
Benson 1969, 12-14

The chief difference in House A.V (fig. 5) between Strata D and E is one of floor levels. The only changes in plan were occasioned when a second wall was built against the inner face of the original northeast wall of Room 1 to reinforce it and, perhaps, when the northwest wall of A.IV.1 was incorporated into House A.V to serve as a shed.

Several of the stone foundations of House A.V were raised or repaired at the beginning of Period E. That a number of walls and foundations collapsed at the end of Period D was shown by the debris of that period, which included in several cases parts of the foundations in addition to the brick of the walls. It was possible to identify the repairs in two places. A course of large, flat stones was added to the northeast foundation of Room 2, and the southwest foundation of Room 4 was almost entirely rebuilt. The new construction here was very poor, with sun-dried bricks even in the foundations.

No fallen debris of Stratum D was found in Rooms 1 and 5. It is possible that there was none, but it is more probable that these rooms collapsed as well and that the debris was completely cleared away. The Period E floors in these two rooms are not distinguished in any way from the many successive habitation levels of this and the preceding period. In fact, we do not know where to draw the line between the deposit of the two periods in Room 5. The floors of the other rooms of the house lay on the smoothed debris of the preceding period. There was some lime on the floor of Room 4, but the other rooms had no special surfacing.

The thresholds of Room 3 were raised to suit the new floor levels. These new thresholds were made of stones, that of the southwest door lying on Period D debris, that of the northwest door resting on the rock. At some later time, perhaps the beginning of Period F, both doorways were closed with rubble masonry, apparently to provide a firm foundation for higher and later walls. No deposit of the later period is preserved in this house.

A large pit was sunk from the Stratum E floor of A.V.2 and cut through the earlier levels. It may have held a pithos. There was a smaller pit at the northwest wall of Room 1. An amphoroid krater (B813) was found in a pit in the courtyard. The platform in the south corner of Room 3 remained in use in Period E, but the pithos lay forgotten under the tumble.

Two bowls of LC IIIA style, one painted (B406) and the other plain (B900), lay on the floor of Room 4. A chalice (B620) was found in the wall debris over the floor and probably stood on a shelf. On the floor of Room 1 were found a jug (B767) and a vat of plain ware (B964). A large undecorated bowl (B811) was found in the debris of Room 5. Like the chalice in Room 4, this must have been standing on a shelf when the house collapsed. Building debris was found in all the rooms, between the tops of the foundations and the Stratum E floors. The closing of the doorways of Room 3 would seem to imply that this room was re-used in the following period, but a large stone basin placed across the foundations of the adjoining Period E walls of A.V.2 and A.VI.3 in Period F shows conclusively that at least these two rooms were not rebuilt. No deposit of Periods F or G was found in House A.V.

A date *post quem* for the reconstruction of House A.V in Period E is furnished by the end of Period D.

HOUSE A.VI (pl. 3a-c)
Benson 1969, 12-14

House A.VI was rebuilt in Period E (fig. 9). The debris occasioned by the collapse at the end of Period D was partly removed and smoothed out; the thresholds in the doorways were raised and new floors were prepared at the new, higher levels. Most of the walls were rebuilt directly on the old foundations, which may have been strengthened at this time.

In Stratum D, the area southwest of House A.VI was occupied by House A.VIa, which was replaced at the beginning of Period E by House A.VIII (see fig. 24). The southwest wall of House A.VI was rebuilt to serve as a party wall for the two houses. In view of the higher level of House A.VIII, it was necessary to increase the height of the stone foundation of the wall joining the two houses. Three to four irregular courses of stones were added at this time and are easily distinguished from the original construction. On the side toward House A.VI, where the masonry of both periods was visible, the addition was carefully made and its face was flush with the earlier wall. On the upper side toward House A.VIII, however, the floor of Period E covered the junction between the two stages in the foundation, so that a neat junction was not necessary. As a result, the southwestern face of the new wall extends beyond its predecessor in some places and rests on earth; in other places it falls several centimeters short of the original wall.

This wall is very important for the relative chronology of the two houses. The facts already mentioned make it clear that its rebuilding was occasioned by the construction of House A.VIII. This conclusion is confirmed by a storage jar which was built against the wall in the eastern corner of A.VIII.3. It is so close to the wall that it cannot have been placed there before the wall was built, yet the paving of the floor runs over the fill in the pit in which the jar was placed and to its rim. It is thus clear that this wall was built prior to the laying of the floor and the finishing of House A.VIII.

That the building of this wall must have coincided with the rebuilding of House A.VI, following the collapse at the end of Period D, is obvious. There is evidence for only one collapse of House A.VI at this time, and it is certain that the house could not have continued to stand while its western wall was fallen and in the process of rebuilding. Direct proof that the rebuilding of the wall—and inferentially the construction of House A.VIII—dates from Period E of House A.VI is furnished by a small oven in the southern corner of A.VI.5. This rests on the Period E floor of the room and is built up against the wall, attached to both the original and the new masonry. The wall was thus rebuilt prior to the construction of the oven, which is clearly associated with the Period E floor in A.VI.5. We can thus only conclude that the building of House A.VIII and the reconstruction of House A.VI at the beginning of Period E were strictly contemporary.

It has already been seen that House A.V was rebuilt when A.VIII was built, so it must be concluded that all three houses were constructed at the same time. That at least Houses A.V and A.VI collapsed at the same time, at the end of Period E, has been demonstrated above. The northeastern part of the two houses, at least, was never rebuilt. The collapse of Houses A.V and A.VI would presumably involve the fall of the neighboring House A.VIII. There is thus justification in saying that the three houses were strictly contemporary in Period E as regards both their construction and their destruction.

When House A.VI was rebuilt, at the beginning of Period E, it was also found necessary to rebuild at least those parts of the northeastern and northwestern walls of A.VI.4 which lay over the LC II pit in the northern corner of Room 4. The pit was dug out to a depth of 0.60 m., and presumably a foundation of Period D was removed. New rubble foundations were then constructed in the line of the walls concerned.

The most important innovation in the plan of House A.VI in Period E is found in Rooms 2 and 5. The deposit of Period D was dug out to the floor along the northwestern walls of these two rooms and heavy rubble foundations were built in both rooms, lying directly on the Period D floors. The foundations vary from 0.90 to 0.95 m. in width; that in A.VI.5 is 2.60 m. long, while that in A.VI.2 is preserved to a length of 1.80 m. The northeastern end of the latter was cut by the disturbance of the Archaic period. Nothing remains of the superstructure in Room 2 and only a few blocks remain in Room 5, of which the most important are two large rectangular blocks which lie side by side at the southwestern end of the foundation. One face of the block nearest the wall to House A.VIII has been pried up in a recent attempt at removal, but the undisturbed face shows that the surface of this block lay about 0.15 m. below that of its neighbor. It is tempting

to restore these blocks as remnants of the two bottom steps of a stairway borne on these foundations. The lower stone may have belonged to a landing which ran the width of the foundation and was entered from the southeast in Room 5. The second block would be one of two or three forming a first step above the landing. A large, irregularly shaped stone 1.60 m. from the wall to House A.VIII has a hole drilled in its upper surface. While it is likely that this stone was removed from elsewhere and that the cutting is of no significance here, it may be that the hole was designed to hold a wooden support which ran up through the superstructure. The foundation ends 1.20 m. short of the doorway to Room 6. From this point to the northeast wall of the room, the stairway, if such it be, must have been borne on beams. An excellent candidate for a supplementary support for this part of the stairway is the rectangular stone post support which lies against the northeast wall of this room exactly in the line of the outer face of the foundation. There is a sinking 0.11 by 0.15 m. in its upper face to keep the post it held from slipping.

Since the northeastern end of the foundation in Room 2 is destroyed, and since nothing remains of the superstructure in that room, it is difficult to interpret what remains. It would not seem to have been related to the stairway.

In discussing the remains of House A.VI in Period D, we found reason to believe that there may have been a second storey over Room 2, but probably none over Room 5. There are similar reasons to think that Room 4 had only one floor in this period. If this is correct, it is probable that all three of the small rooms along the northeastern side of the house had second storeys, whereas the large rooms did not.

The oven in the south corner of Room 5 has already been mentioned. It was 0.55 m. wide, 0.70 m. long, and at least 0.40 m. high, reaching to the preserved top of the southwestern wall of the house. The oven was built of sun-dried bricks, placed against the southwestern and southeastern walls of the room. There was a door, 0.15 m. wide, in the middle of the northwestern side of the oven. Its interior was covered by a thick coating of clay, which extended out the door and onto a large stone which lay on the floor in front of it. The oven was found full of ashes, which must have accumulated in the last days of the house's use. In these ashes were found many sherds of a Proto-White Painted amphoriskos (B663), some of which were burned. Other sherds of the same vase were found on the floor of Room 4, directly under fallen roof debris. These circumstances show that this important vase was in use within a few days, or even hours, of the destruction of the house. Some sherds of another Proto-White Painted vase (B669) which were embedded in the clay with which the oven was lined joined fragments found in Pit 2 in Room 6, which was closed before the end of Period E.

Two pits and a built fireplace in Room 6 could be arranged in chronological order. The earliest was Pit 2, a large shallow pit which must have been closed well before the end of Period E. This contained fragments of the two Proto-White Painted vases, B669, mentioned above, and B622. Pit 1 cut through the fill of Pit 2, and is thus of later date. Pit 1 is a shallow unlined pit which was filled with ashes. It may have served as a fireplace. Toward the end of Period E, a more refined fireplace was built over Pit 1. A shallow depression was scooped out of the ashes and lined with clay. Three rows of stones were erected in a circle back of it and a small ash pit was dug out in front and faced with clay. This was separated from the fireplace proper by a narrow ridge of clay. The region between the fireplace and the southwestern wall of the room was filled with miscellaneous brick rubble to the level of the top of the fireplace. This appears to be debris of Period D which was not cleared off at the beginning of Period E. Perhaps it was related to predecessors of the fireplace which are not preserved. The fireplace remained in use until the end of Period E.

A pit 0.70 m. deep was sunk from the Period E floor in Room 5; building debris in its upper half indicates that it was open when the house collapsed. The grey, sandy earth in the bottom contained numerous Proto-White Painted sherds, including B628, 627 and 661. A pit against the northeastern wall of Room 3 contained three Proto-White Painted sherds (B626, 689).

The Period E floors of Rooms 2, 4 and 6 consisted of the Period D debris, smoothed out, packed and coated with lime. A layer of pure *chavara,* 0.20 m. deep, was laid in Room 3. In Room 5, the floor was covered by large flat flag-

stones, laid in mortar of clay, lime and *chavara,* placed over the earlier debris. This floor was well preserved in the southwestern part of the room and the imprint of the flagstones could be seen in the mortar in a number of places where the stones themselves were missing. The excavation during the Archaic period badly disturbed the northeastern part of the house, but there is no good reason to doubt that the pavement extended over the entire room.

The higher floor levels of Period E called for higher thresholds. That of the wide door between Rooms 2 and 5 was raised, using a row of river stones, and that between Rooms 5 and 6 was finished with large flat limestone blocks.

Over the Period E floors of Rooms 2 and 5 there were 0.03 to 0.04 m. of accumulation. In the other rooms the building debris lay directly on the floors. Some 0.10 m. of *konnos* lay directly on the floor of Room 4, and directly below the usual wall debris. This was pure except for moderate traces of vegetable matter, identical with that found over the Period D floor of A.VI.5, and there identified as fallen roof matter. The traces of vegetable matter found in the *konnos* in Room 4 perhaps came from the matting or thatching on which the roof lay. This, again, is an indication that there was no second storey over Room 4. On the floor under the roof debris were found fragments of three Proto-White Painted pots (B669, 677, 682).

The house collapsed at the end of Period E, and the northeastern walls fell out into the street. These were never cleared off and this part of the house was thenceforth abandoned.

HOUSE A.VIII (pls. 4d; 5a-c)
Benson 1969, 13-15

House A.VIII was first constructed in Period E, replacing House A.VIa, but Rooms 1 and 5 of A.VIII extended beyond the limits of the earlier house; on the other hand, Room 2 of House A.VIa seems not to have fallen within the area of A.VIII, but rather became part of its courtyard.

Since the construction of House A.VIII dates from LC IIIB, a time when the Proto-White Painted style of pottery was beginning to appear and when there were other signs of a new ethnic accretion in Cyprus, it might be thought that the new house perhaps belonged to the newcomers. In this connection, it is interesting to note that House A.VIII adheres to the typical L-shaped plan of the preceding period, which is by now characteristically Cypriote and finds no parallel in contemporary architecture of the Greek mainland (see *infra* pp. 58-59). This house is, in fact, an unusually good example of the L-shaped plan. Whether or not the angle was filled by a room or series of rooms remains unknown, though a stub wall projecting slightly northwestward from the west corner of A.VIII.1 suggests that such a room, or rooms, did exist. The stub wall consists of only a single course of stones on bedrock and may have been a later addition rather than part of the original plan.

The southwestern parts of all rooms except 2 lie on bedrock; the northeastern parts lie over earlier deposit. There was none of the careful quarrying characteristic of the wave of construction at the beginning of Period D. Room 2 lay over the scanty remains of A.VIa.1. The deposit under the northeastern end of Rooms 3 and 4 goes back into the LC II period; deposit of the LC Ia period was found in the outside angle of the northwestern wall of Room 1 and the southwestern wall of Room 3. The early wall of which traces remain under the southwestern side of Rooms 3 and 4 formed part of House A.VIa.

The northwestern walls of Rooms 3 and 5 lie on rock in the southwest, but on earlier accumulation in the northeast. The northwestern and southwestern walls of Room 2 lie in part on rock, in part on the stubs of the earlier walls of A.VIa.1. All the other walls of the house are founded entirely on the bedrock. The wall between Rooms 4 and 5 lies in a deep foundation trench on the side of Room 4. The upper course of the northwestern wall of Room 1 is wider than the lower course; this must represent a rebuilding subsequent to Period E.

In Room 3 all the walls were coated with lime. There is no such evidence for other rooms of the house, though such a coating is not improbable.

A.VIII.1 was the largest room of the house (pl. 4d) and appears to have played an important role in the household economy. A large bin of brick and stone stood against the northwestern wall and may have served as a temporary receptacle for the meal which was ground on the large saddle quern which lay on the floor in front of it.

Another smaller quern lay among pithos fragments in the center of the room, close to a large flat stone embedded in the floor, which may have held a wooden support for the ceiling. There was a doorway in each of three of the walls of the room, none in the southwestern wall. A doorway led from the eastern corner of the room into what appears to have been a courtyard. The doorway is 1.20 m. wide and is bounded on the southwest by a large block of calcareous sandstone, which stands on end. It was probably matched by another similar block on the outer face of the wall. The interesting feature of this block, which measures 0.60 by 0.32 by 0.15 m., is that it appears to have been cut with a saw.[10] An unpretentious doorway, 0.65 m. wide, led from the eastern corner of the room down into Room 2. A step was provided by leaving part of the brick superstructure of the Period D wall standing on its foundation. Since the earlier wall lies somewhat northeast of the Period E wall, it forms a convenient, if inelegant, step. The doorway which led from Room 3 up into Room 1, which was on a higher level, was an opening 1.15 m. wide. The floor level of Room 3 continued 0.15 m. into the opening. At this point the floor rose to the level of that in Room 1. Forming the step was a rubble wall ca. 0.40 m. thick, set into a cutting in rock which continues the line of the southeast side of the wall between Rooms 1 and 3, and rising almost to the level of the floor of Room 1. The plaster coating seems to have run continuously from the floor of Room 3, up the face of this filling wall and onto the floor of Room 1. On the face of the filling wall, the plaster filled the interstices, and large chunks of it remain.

The western corner of Room 3 and at least half the length of its southwestern wall was occupied by an elaborately built structure of stone and brick, which lay directly over the wall foundation of A.VIa (pl. 5a). This structure consists of a narrow stone wall, 0.23 m. wide, built against the outer wall of room 3; parallel to this, and ca. 0.30 m. in front of it, is a row of bricks standing on their long sides. Some of the stones of the foundation of House A.VIa were removed here to give greater depth to the pit thus formed; the pit in

---

10. On the sawing of stone blocks, see Petrie 1923, 72-74; Forbes 1964, 130.

turn was lined with plaster, which went over the top of both stone and brick walls and probably was continuous with the plaster of the first floor. In the west corner of the room, the structure abutted against the cross wall between Rooms 3 and 4 and the heavy plaster coating of the wall formed the end of the rectangular pit. It is not certain how far across the southwestern side of the room it went, but the excavator observed that the plaster was missing from the lower part of this wall right up to the step in the doorway; so it may have gone all across the room, in which case it would have obstructed part of the doorway between Rooms 1 and 3. Since this structure, however, seems originally not to have extended very far above the floor, it may actually have served as a step in the doorway. It is indicated on the plan only as now preserved. The second floor of Room 3 seems to have gone right over the whole structure, but above the structure both the stone back wall and another brick wall were built up in an exactly similar manner and the pit again lined with plaster. The third floor of this room, which finally brought it even with the floor of Room 1, seems to have covered over the structure, and there is no evidence of a second rebuilding over it. The structure seems thus to have been a most carefully prepared, perhaps waterproof, container of size and type unparalleled in Bamboula. It would probably have been covered and thus also served as a low bench, and in part as a step, as suggested.

The amphoroid krater of plain ware (B947) which stood in the pit in the eastern corner of Room 3 (pl. 5b) was mentioned above in connection with the date of the party wall of Houses A.VIII and A.VI. The pit in which the krater was placed cut the foundation trenches of both the first and second phases of the wall, and the belly of the pot actually projected slightly under the upper courses. The mouth of the pot lay some 0.10 m. below the prevailing floor level. The floor is scooped out around the mouth, and the lime surfacing of the floor slopes down to it. The vase is thus clearly associated with both the floor and the reconstruction of the party wall with House A.VI.

A flat stone embedded in the floor in the approximate center of Room 3 was probably a base for a wooden support for the ceiling. Much pottery lay on the accumulation over the floor of Room 3 and was crushed in place when the house collapsed—B621, 814, 819, 820, 863, 899, 914, 949.

The northeast end of the wall between Rooms 2 and 3 was damaged by a recent intrusion, so that the doorway which once stood in this place is only partly preserved. In the 0.40 m. nearest the northeast wall of the house, the intrusion went to just below the level of the Period E floor. In the undisturbed earth below this, no stones were found, so it is improbable that the wall went this far. Some 0.40 m. from the northeast wall, a rectangular block, 0.10 by 0.30 m., straddles the wall, falling somewhat short of either face. This is adjoined on the southwest by a large flat block which extends the full width of the wall and is about 0.60 m. long—the masonry of the following period has not been removed, so that the exact length of this block is not known. These two flat stones, plus one or more others which stood in the part damaged by the intrusion, form the threshold of the doorway which connected Rooms 2 and 3 in Period E; the doorway was about 1.10 m. wide.

If there were any doubt of the contemporaneity of the destruction of Rooms 2 and 3, it would be removed by the fact that one piece of a pot (B819) was found on the accumulation in Room 2, while the rest of the vase was found crushed on the floor of Room 3.

A number of pots of plain ware stood on the floor of A.VIII.4 when the house fell. Because of the subsequent disturbance in this room, however, not enough of any one pot was found to make it possible to mend it. The traces of the earlier wall of A.VIa, which ran along the southwest end of Room 4, have already been mentioned. These traces consist of a number of unhewn stones, probably of a leveling course, set in a foundation trench. Owing to the poor preservation of this room, it was not possible to say whether the Period E floor covered these or not.

A large stone at the northeast end of the wall between Rooms 4 and 5 is one jamb of the doorway which connected these two rooms at the time of Period E. It has not been possible to locate the other side of the doorway. The doorway was walled up after the collapse of the house at the end of the Period E, and Room 5 was not rebuilt.

Room 4 was connected with Room 3 by a simple doorway about a meter wide at the northeastern end of their party wall. There was no built threshold; the flooring of Room 3 ran through it. If there was a room or rooms in the angle of this house, entrance to it (or them) must have been from Room 4, for entrances from both Rooms 1 and 3 are precluded by the preserved walls. As is customary in such L-shaped houses, a room or rooms in the angle would fall short of Room 5, with the result that there would barely be space for a doorway in the southwest wall of Room 4, which is totally destroyed. Thus, despite the stub of a wall extending to the northwest from the west corner of Room 1, filling of the angle seems unlikely.

A low clay platform lay against the northeast wall of Room 5 and a double bin stood in the south corner of the room (pl. 5c). The eastern half of the bin is built of sun-dried brick. The western half is enclosed on two sides by the house walls, on the third side by the brick bin, and on the fourth by a low coping of clay. This half of the bin is completely coated with a very thin layer of *chavara* plaster, like that commonly used for flooring. Two flat stones were embedded in the floor of Room 5. One of these, in front of the bins, has a deep hole bored into the top (pl. 5c); the purpose of this is not clear. Since it was covered by the fragments of a vase (B850), it is clear that it was not supporting anything when the house collapsed. A large rectangular stone placed on edge in the center of the room was a post support. Other supports of similar shape were found in Houses A.VII.3 and D.I.1. Fragments of several vases (B849, 850, 948) lay on the accumulation in Room 5.

The preserved rooms of House A.VIII had floors coated with lime; that of Room 3 was continuous with the lime surfacing of the walls. The floor material went down into the foundation trenches of the walls in this room.

A thick layer of crushed limestone was thrown in over the ruins of the southwest wall of A.VIa.2 to level off the courtyard and give it a mud-free surface. This merges with the bedrock, which rises sharply in the southwest. The designation of this area as a courtyard is indicated by the lack of walls enclosing it on the northeast, southeast, or southwest, as well as by parallels furnished by

other houses of the same plan. Some fragments of storage pottery were found on the pavement near the door to Room 1. The deposit over the floor of the courtyard was entirely disturbed.

Over the floors of all the rooms of House A.VIII lay an accumulation from 0.003 to 0.007 m. thick; in Room 2 it reached a depth of 0.11 m. Most of the pottery found in the house lay on this accumulation, crushed by the walls of the house which collapsed at the end of Period E. Building debris of Period E lay to a depth of 0.29 m. in Room 1, 0.14 m. in Room 2, 0.13 m. in Room 3, and 0.43 m. in Room 5. The unusual depth in the last room is due to the fact that this room was not rebuilt in Period F, so that the debris was not cleared off.

Data which establish the relative chronology of the houses in Period E have been mentioned in passing and may here be summarized briefly. The crucial evidence for the beginning of the period is the wall which forms the northeast boundary of House A.VIII and is shared with Houses A.V and A.VI. This wall had collapsed at the end of Period D and was rebuilt at the beginning of Period E. Though sufficient height was preserved on the original foundation for House A.VI, the foundation was not high enough for the floors of the new house, A.VIII, to the southwest. As a result, several more courses were added to the foundation to bring it up to the floor level of the new house. The date of this wall relative to the houses of Period E is established by the following points: (1) It immediately follows the collapse of the houses of Period E. This is shown in A.V.4. The part of the wall which falls within this room was rebuilt. In order to do this, the debris of Period D was dug out to the level of the floor in the neighboring A.VIII.5 and the reconstruction was begun at this level. The fact that the foundation was not carried to the bottom of the Period D debris in A.V.4 shows that the reconstruction was subsequent to that stratum. (2) That the rebuilt foundation was used during Period E of House A.VI is shown by the oven which stands on the Period E floor of A.VI.5, and which is built up against both the original and the reconstructed foundations of the wall in question. (3) That this foundation antedates the use of House A.VIII, but was built as part of the original plan of that house, is shown by its relation to the floor in that room. A storage jar which was placed so close to the wall that it could not possibly date from a period prior to the reconstruction was sunk in a pit which was covered by the original floor of the room. This floor runs to the reconstructed foundation, and the material of which the floor was made goes into the foundation trench for the wall. From these three points we conclude with certainty that the original construction of House A.VIII was strictly contemporary with the reconstruction of Houses A.V and A.VI.

That Houses A.V and A.VI collapsed at the same time at the end of Period E is shown by the fact that the debris from the two houses covered the same thin stratum in the street, and that one fragment of a Proto-White Painted vase was found on the street under the debris of House A.V, while another fragment of the same vase was found under the debris of House A.VI. That the northeast part of both houses remained in ruins after Period E is shown by the large stone basin which lies across the joint foundations of both houses.

While there is no direct stratigraphical proof that House A.VIII collapsed at exactly the same time as A.V and A.VI, it is altogether probable that it did, since they shared party walls, so that the collapse of two houses would probably entail that of the third. This conclusion is strengthened by general archaeological considerations, chief of which is the fact that the subsequent rebuilding of House A.VIII corresponds with that of the

southwest part of House A.VI.

All the decorated pottery found *in situ* in House A.VI was of the Proto-White Painted style, whereas no vases of this style were found in Houses A.V and A.VIII. That the ware was known when the houses were constructed is shown by the presence of a sherd of this style under the lime floor in A.VIII.3, and of eight sherds of a contemporary ware in the stairway foundation in A.VI.5. Sherds of the same ware found in the debris from the walls in both Houses A.V and A.VIII likely belong to the material built into the walls, and in that case also date from the construction of the house. That the Proto-White Painted ware was in use prior to the destruction of House A.V is shown by the sherd which was found on the street under the debris of the house, as well as by numerous other sherds in the successive repavings of the street prior to the collapse of the house, and in the contemporary deposit between the street and the Circuit Wall. A painted bowl (B406) from A.V.4 should perhaps be classified as Proto-White Painted, while two plain vases (B914, 948) in House A.VIII perhaps show Proto-White Painted influence.

The Proto-White Painted ware was thus known at the beginning of Period E, when it was produced side by side with the ware typical of the previous period. The markedly different proportions of the two wares in the different houses is probably due to different personal tastes; it is not indicative of a chronological difference.

STRATUM F

Benson 1969, 15

The reduction in the inhabited area on Bamboula which was noted in Period E became much more marked in Period F. The earlier reduction shows a definite shift of population to another region, probably nearer to the sea and not far from the contemporary Kaloriziki cemetery; the second loss of population practically ended the history of Bamboula as a densely populated district, and we are dealing only with isolated houses among the ruins of the earlier city.

At the beginning of Period F, six and probably seven adjacent rooms were rebuilt in the excavated area. It is of interest to note that the rooms which survive do not form the entirety of any one

house of the preceding period (fig. 11). Room 5 is lost from House A.VIII, and Rooms 1, 2 and 3 from House A.VI. No part of House A.V was certainly rebuilt, though the walling up of the doors of Room 3 may well belong to this stratum. This redistribution of rooms raises the question of whether we are dealing with restricted survivals of the several earlier houses, still inhabited by their former inhabitants, or whether these had by now moved to the new site and the ruins of parts of two houses were rebuilt to form a single unit, with a change of ownership. The absence of doorways in the party wall between Houses A.VI and A.VIII suggests that the two houses were still separate. The same conclusion is indicated by the number of rooms which we know were rebuilt; a six- or seven-room house seems improbable in a period of marked curtailment.

It is not unlikely that more of the area was inhabited at this time than the remains indicate. Strata F and G are very close to the present surface of the land, and it is only good fortune that has preserved as much as we have. But even if the settlement were more extensive, it was not sufficiently so to alter seriously the picture presented by the preserved ruins.

The Stratum E building debris northeast of A.VI.4, 5 and 6 was left as it fell and gradually became covered with drift. A large stone basin was placed on the ruins of the northeast foundation at the junction of Houses A.V and A.VI.

In the rooms shown in fig. 11 the Period E debris was smoothed out, part of it being removed, some of the foundations and presumably all of the walls were rebuilt, and new floors were laid. Much sand was found on the floor of A.VI.5, and patches of ash were found in both this room and A.VI.6. The upper part of the Stratum E oven in A.VI.5, which projected above the debris, was covered with clay and used as a fireplace at the new level. The foundation of the stairway was still visible, but in view of the abandonment of

A.VI.2, it is improbable that the stairway was still used. Many stone implements, saddle querns, pestles, rubbers and the like, were found on this floor.

The southeast foundation of A.VIII.3 was raised at the beginning of Period F. The doorway into Room 2 was filled with rubble up to the level of the new floor and a threshold was made of white clay, similar to that used in roofing. The floor and walls were again coated with lime. The long rectangular pit along the southwest wall of the room was rebuilt on the new floor. The threshold of the doorway into Room 4 was raised by the addition of a single course of stones.

A new floor was prepared over the debris in A.VIII.1 and surfaced with gravel. The bin against the northwest wall continued in use. A stone grinder was found on this floor. The floors of Rooms A.VIII.2 and 4 were not preserved. The use of these rooms at this time is inferred from the fact that the doorways which gave access to them were reconstructed. It is uncertain whether A.VI.4 was rebuilt or not.

The house, or houses, again collapsed at the end of Period F, as is shown by building debris found in Rooms A.VI.5 and 6 and A.VIII.4 and 3.

STRATUM G

Benson 1969, 15

Slight traces of Stratum G were found over the Stratum F deposit in A.VI.5 and 6 and A.VIII.1 and 3. It may well be that the other rooms of Period F remained in use at this time, but no trace of this last and highest level was found elsewhere on Bamboula. Owing to the shallowness of the deposit and the disturbance of the site at the hands of treasure hunters, the remains of this stratum are very slight. What little we have, however, seems to indicate that it was a full-fledged building period comparable with the others discussed above.

The Period G floor in A.VIII.3 consisted, as in the previous periods, of a coating of lime laid over the smoothed debris and fusing with the lime finish of the walls. In this period, the flooring seems to have covered over the long, rectangular, built structure in the southwest corner; at least there is no evidence for a second rebuilding. The level of

this third floor in A.VIII.3 was now about the same as that in A.VIII.1, eliminating the step between them. Room A.VIII.3 was disturbed to what remains of the Stratum G floor, so no ancient deposit was found *in situ*.

In Room A.VIII.1, the debris was smoothed out and packed and used as a floor without special surfacing. A large stone slab was placed in front of the doorway to A.VIII.3. The bin in the western corner of the room had by now filled up and lost its previous function; what little appeared above the new floor was pressed into service as a pot stand. A bowl (B527) and the fragments of a pithos were found lying on and near it; a stone grinder (B1491) lay near by. Over this floor lay 0.22 m. of stone and brick tumble, which reached up to the level of the plowed land which, unfortunately, was badly disturbed.

Traces of Stratum G floors were discovered as well in the southwestern part of A.VI.5 and 6.

There was some gravel on the floor of A.VI.5; the floor of A.VI.6 consisted simply of the smoothed tumble. Some 0.15 m. of sandy earth containing a great deal of ash were found over these floors and there was a bit of brick tumble over this in

A.VI.5.

No attempt was made to clear off the building debris over Stratum G, for this was the last habitation level of the early settlement and the site remained uninhabited henceforth.

CIRCUIT WALL

Benson 1970, 25-29

Important remains of a Circuit Wall were discovered on the northeast slope of Bamboula, largely in the southeastern third of Area A (fig. 1, fig. 24) and some distance up the hill from the sharp drop below the 77-meter contour line. The wall continued north-northwestward, coming somewhat closer to the bluff, across the central part of Area A. It apparently continued beyond the northwesternmost point excavated, but there are no surface indications of its either crossing the old Limassol-Paphos road or turning westward around the knoll of Bamboula. Nor has the wall been traced southeast of the southeasternmost point excavated. Here the bluff is quite high, so that a moderate-sized wall on top of it would probably have been sufficient for defense. Near the southeasternmost point excavated, the wall jogs from south-southeast more to the southeast (point *i* on fig. 24) and it may have approached the bluff and run along it; on the other hand, it may have stopped where it met the rock escarpment.

The wall, as mentioned, does not lie at the edge of the field; rather, it is ca. 24 m. from it at the southeasternmost point excavated; the northeast tower is 15 m. from the edge, and the wall running northwest from the tower is roughly 7 m. from it. There is no explanation for the great accumulation of earth, some 3 m., at the edge and its sudden drop to the lower land to the northeast. It would appear likely that there was a second fortification wall here, but no trace of this is visible in the bank, and our exploratory trench, which came as close as possible to the irrigation ditch that runs along the edge of the field, revealed no such traces. The deep deposit of earth which runs from the wall to the present edge of the field is of Late Roman or still later date. It seems that the terrain in the Late Bronze Age ran almost level from the base of the wall into the fields to the northeast.

The excavations have revealed three sections of the wall, covering a total length of 93 m., if we include two faces of the tower and count the unexcavated sections as continuing in a straight line. These three sections are: the tower of the Late Bronze Age, towers of the Archaic period and the lengths of walls of both periods that run to the southeast and northwest of the tower(s). The excavated remains fall into the two main chronological groups just mentioned, one of the Late Bronze Age, the other of the Archaic period, with subsequent remodelings running down into early Imperial times. Most of the visible remains belong to the reconstruction(s) of the Archaic period, carried out on a large scale, if in poor style. The Archaic masonry is very uneven and shaky. It consists of an outer face of large unhewn blocks and a broad fill of miscellaneous stones and some earth thrown in behind it. Owing to the great breadth of this, averaging 2.50 m., it is improbable that the brick superstructure covered more than about half; the rest may have served as a paved road.

The remains of the Late Bronze Age are easily recognized by their much more regular masonry, as well as by the fact that they often lie under the later wall. In most cases, it was not deemed advisable to remove the later wall so as to study its predecessor in detail, but cuts were made through it in the central part of Area A during the original excavations of 1937-1939; a section at the extreme southeastern end of the excavated part was investigated in 1941 and again in 1948, when the staircase at point *j* on fig. 24 was disclosed; this was investigated further in 1951, at which time elucidation of the masonry within the towers was sought.

In the southeastern section, the walls of the two periods are distinct, the Archaic structure lying to the northeast of that of the Late Bronze Age (pl. 6a). The Late Bronze Age wall here is a terrace wall lying a short distance from the rock escarpment and retaining a mass of earth and rubble. The wall proper is 0.75 to 1.40 m. thick, carefully built of unhewn, but roughly rectangular blocks, laid without mortar of any sort (pl. 6b). For the first 5.50 m., the wall runs in a straight line to the northwest; it then turns 35 degrees to the north and continues for 4.00 m., after which it is lost on the surface. At its beginning in the southeast, this wall rests in part on bedrock, in part on a thin layer of red clay over the rock. In the area of the bend, the LC wall rests in part on the red clay layer and in part on gravelly hardpan.

The Archaic wall lies 0.80 m. in front of the early wall at the southeasternmost point excavated, 2.00 m. at the angle of the early wall (point *i*) and 1.50 m. at the northwesternmost end of the preserved Bronze Age wall. The Archaic wall lies in part on rock, in part on earth over the rock. No foundation trench was cut for it, but in places the rock was cut back to form a shelf on which the wall rests. Both here and in the section northwest of the towers, it is built as a terrace wall. The outer face consists of long, unhewn stones laid with their ends out (pl. 6c). This facing retains an unordered mass of stones, which runs in the southeastern part over the foundations of the earlier wall and to the escarpment. This foundation is rough and irregular and has collapsed in many places, a far cry from the neat work of the previous age. The stone foundation probably rose to a height of about 1.50 m., as in the section in the central part of Area A, and carried a superstructure of sun-dried brick, the height of which can only be surmised.

Just to the southwest of the point where the Late Bronze Age wall met the escarpment, a brick staircase was built, using the rock as its southeast side (point *j* on fig. 24). The other sides of the staircase are built of brick on a stone foundation (pl. 6d). A flight of steps ran up from southwest to northeast (pl. 6e). Four steps are preserved as excavated, and a fifth was removed; they were 0.90 m. wide, had treads varying from 0.35 m. near the bottom to 0.22 m. at the uppermost preserved step, and had risers of 0.25 m. or slightly more. A flattish gray stone was fixed to the bottom step with a clayey plaster, its face flush with the edge of the step. The other steps were covered with a similar plaster, and an unusually large number of natural flat stones were found in the tumble, many of which may have formed the tread of steps. The staircase is filled with earth containing a high percentage of pebbly *chavara* and it is clear that this fill was laid layer by layer as the staircase was built up. It is now preserved 1.35 m. above the floor alongside it, but it must originally have risen to a parapet walk along the inside of the Late Bronze Age Circuit Wall. A total of eight steps would have brought the flight to the northeast outer edge of the staircase, which with nine risers would have had a height of ca. 2.25 m. to the parapet walk; because of the irregularity in the width of the treads, there may have been one step more or less, making the height of the parapet walk vary from 2.00 to 2.50 m. above the floor level. The wall itself might have been another 2.00 m. higher.

Two large foundations were found at the place where the line of the Circuit Wall breaks (pl. 7a); here the section to the northwest of these foundations is ca. 9.00 m. to the northeast of the line of the wall that runs southeast from these foundations. One of these foundations, that to the northeast, is trapezoidal in shape and has maximum dimensions of ca. 8.50 m. both southwest-northeast and southeast-northwest; it is the foundation of a tower. This belongs at least in part to the early fortifications of the Late Bronze Age and was rebuilt in the Archaic period. The foundation lies on bedrock and is bonded to the northwestern section of the Archaic wall (pl. 7b). Two stages are distinguishable in the masonry of the tower. The lower courses were well built and have an even face. The upper part is of the careless construction characteristic of the Archaic structure. The Archaic northeastern face of the tower lies as much as 0.50 m. back from the face of the earlier foundation (pl. 7c). The Archaic fill back of the rebuilt northwestern section of the wall runs up against the northwestern face of the tower, showing that it is later than the original construction of the tower. In all probability, at least the lower courses of the northeast face of this tower remain from the Late Bronze Age fortification.

A second large tower adjoins this on the southwest. Its northwestern face is parallel to that of the outer tower (pl. 7a). This large foundation rests on Archaic earth which filled up against the outer tower after its construction; the inner tower is thus the later of the two and belongs entirely to the later Archaic rebuilding. Only its northeastern and northwestern faces have been excavated; the southwestern face seems to have been lost on the surface. The northeastern face continues the line of the southeastern section of the Archaic wall and rises above the foundation of the outer tower. The excavated remains indicate that this later foundation was roughly rectangular and measured 7.20 m. by 9.00 m. It is built in the usual Archaic manner, with only a single outer row of ordered stones, retaining a heterogeneous mass of rubble. Since it rests on earth rather than on bedrock, its stability would seem questionable were it not for its huge bulk. In all probability, this too was the foundation for a tower.

A section of the Circuit Wall 17.80 m. long was excavated along the northeastern edge of the middle section of Area A (pl. 7d). A strip about 1.80 m. wide was cleared alongside the outer face of the wall in this area and another trench was dug at right angles to this, running from the wall to just before the irrigation ditch at the edge of the hill. This was done in the expectation of finding a second wall at the edge of the hill, which would account for the great depth of artificial fill outside the wall. This hope was not fulfilled. A second wall, however, could exist under the irrigation ditch, but this was nowhere investigated.

The section of the Circuit Wall to the northwest of the towers shows the same extensive remodelling as do the towers and the wall to the southeast of them. In the area marked *a* on fig. 24, the late stone foundations were removed in order to ascertain their date and to learn more exactly the nature of the early wall beneath them.

The original Circuit Wall in this area lay on a shelf cut into the bedrock, which rose to the southwest. The wall was 0.90 m. wide and was of careful rubble construction, built of unhewn but fairly regular blocks. In contrast to the later wall, it had regular faces on both exterior and interior. The preservation of the original wall varies considerably; in the part cleared it rises three or four courses above the rock on the southwest.

The Circuit Wall was more probably constructed first in LC II (Benson 1970, 26). Nothing indicates any change in the wall during the Late Bronze Age, which is marked only by the accumulation of some 0.25 to 0.30 m. of earth in the area behind the wall, which fell into ruins

when Bamboula was abandoned at the end of the LC III period.

Daniel had speculated on the possible existence of a gate in the Circuit Wall, most likely in the area of the towers, but had concluded that there was insufficient evidence to support the supposition. With this possibility in mind, but without being able to do any further excavating, I examined anew the remains of possibly earlier structures within the towers, on the basis of which I should like to put forward here a tentative new interpretation which would support the existence of a gateway.

Within each tower (fig. 24) there is a mass of masonry which apparently antedates the great Archaic tower foundations. The clearest of these is the line of masonry at *e-f*, some 4.15 m. long, with a large roughly squared stone at *e* forming a possible corner. At right angles to this line is that marked *d*, at each end of which is a large squared block (pl. 7e), the total length of *d* being ca. 5.25 m.; if extended to face *e-f*, the length would be ca. 6.00 m. There is no recognizable northwest face to this mass, nor a southwest face, other than that of the large corner block; as preserved, the mass is ca. 1.80 m. wide at the northeast, 1.40 m. at the southwest. It is to be noted that the Late Bronze Age wall, after bending 35 degrees at point *i*, assumes a direction which if extended would bring the outer face of the wall to point *f*. A corresponding mass of masonry in the northwest tower exists at *b* (pl. 7f), but it has no clearly recognizable face on any side; its greatest width is roughly 2.00 m. This may, however, be connected with the rise along the northeast cut at *c*, which is parallel to the line of masonry at *e-f* and ca. 2.50 m. from it. A face similar to that at *e-f* may have existed along this cut, forming the southwest face of the masonry mass in the northeast tower. If this mass were extended to meet the line of Late Bronze Age masonry in the northeast face of this tower, its length would be ca. 6.50 m., only 0.50 m. longer than the corresponding mass in the southwest tower. One can thus reconstruct a gate ca. 2.50 m. wide between two heavy stone bastions, the wall leading up to the southwest bastion at its northwest face, the wall to the northwest running off from the northeast end of the bastion northeast of the gate (fig. 12). The street leading through such a gate would then have run roughly parallel with the wall at just the same distance from it as does the street which has been excavated in the central section of Area A (fig. 24). Only further excavation can indicate the validity of the proposed gateway, which may have existed as part of the Late Bronze Age fortifications.

The Archaic rebuilding of the fortification system seems to have taken place in at least two phases, for the southwest tower is clearly added to the northwest tower; the interval may not have been great. This is Benson's stage IV in the history of the wall (Benson 1970, 27). There is then evidence for some rebuilding of the wall in the sixth century B.C. (Phase V). This was apparently a large-scale operation, which was largely responsible for the poor preservation of the early parts of the wall. A large area back of the wall was cleared in preparation for this reconstruction, disturbing much of the earlier fill right down to bedrock. In the wall itself, much of the masonry was removed down to the top of the preserved masonry of the Late Bronze Age wall. The wall was then rebuilt with only the outer face laid regularly, with large unhewn blocks laid end out; behind this was an unordered pack of stones, approximately level on top and with an average width of 2.50 m.

A shallow cutting containing Hellenistic sherds was observed in a few places at the northwestern edge of the sixth-century wall (Phase VI), but it is not certain that this represents an attempt to rebuild the wall. The wall was rebuilt for the last time in the first or second century after Christ (Phase VII). Sherds of eastern red-glazed pottery, formerly known as Pergamene ware, and other contemporary wares are associated with a few courses of stone on the top of the preserved wall. These courses are rather irregular and do not follow the earlier foundation exactly; in one place they run 0.45 m. to the northwest. This wall varied from 1.20 m. to 1.50 m. wide and was built with two moderately regular faces, filled between with stones and earth. As in the other stages of the wall, nothing was preserved of the superstructure.

The date at which the wall was finally abandoned and the area outside it filled up to the present level can be determined only approximately. The presence of Late Roman wares on the bedrock indicates that this took place not before the third or fourth century after Christ. The absence of Byzantine glazed ware gives an upper limit. The wall was perhaps abandoned in the bleak years which followed the destruction of Kourion by earthquake in the latter part of the fourth century.

CHAPTER III

AREAS B AND D

AREA B

TRENCH 11—THE WELL (pl. 8a-d)
Benson 1969, 15; 1970, 29-30

During the second season of excavations at Bamboula, 1938, Daniel began to dig at the top of the hill (fig. 1), opening Trench 11 a little below and to the southwest of the threshing floor (fig. 13); it was 62 m. long and 1.50 m. wide. In it was discovered the great square well, around which the trench was widened to 6 m. to allow its proper investigation. No other walls were found in the long trench.

The well was found to be 1.80 m. square in its upper, built part; its corners are oriented to the cardinal points. The highest stone still in place, in the northeast face of the well, was at −2.91 m. below datum. The preserved top then sloped down to the southwest, with the slope of the hill, but the full square became evident about 0.70 m. lower down (pl. 8a). The masonry walls, solidly built of rather flat slabs of stone, each with a straight edge in the face of the wall, descended to −8.60 to −9.60 m. (pl. 8b), where they rested on rock, and below this the shaft was cut into the solid rock to −20.96 m., for a total depth of 18.05 m. The well was excavated to the bottom, which was cleared; but water occurred in the lowest part. For some 10.0 m. above the floor of the well, the fill was apparently an accumulation dating to Geometric and early Archaic times. For the next meter, the fill seems to have been brought in to close the well. In with this fill was an enormous stone, 1.85 m. long, while above this fill large pieces of *chavara* occurred and among them another very large stone, 11.50 m. long by 0.50 m. wide by 0.25 m. thick, at the upper edges of which are many grooves worn by the ropes used to lower receptacles into the well (pl. 8c). This must have fallen from the top of the well after it went out of use. Indeed, most of the fill of the well in the upper 4.0 m. of the preserved shaft was comprised of the collapsed masonry from the destroyed part of the shaft. Much of this material was used to reconstruct the upper part of the shaft (pl. 8d), in order to strengthen and preserve it.

On the basis of the sherds found in the foundation trench for the well wall, the construction of the well can be dated to the LC II period (Benson 1969, 15). It can be assumed to have been in use through LC III, as well as during the Geometric and Early Archaic periods, after which it was put out of use by a fill dumped into the shaft.

TRENCH 15
Benson 1969, 16

Farther down Bamboula and to the west of the well, Trench 15 was dug first for a length of 6.0 m. and a width of 1.50 m., but was enlarged when house remains were found in the eastern end of the original cut. The main part of the trench was eventually 11.0 m. by 8.50 m. (fig. 14).

The architectural remains are too scanty for detailed analysis, and little information on them has been recorded, but they do indicate that houses were built fairly close to the top of the hill. There seem to be part of one house (Units 1 and 4), possibly a narrow street down the slope of the hill (2), and a small part of another house on the east side of the street (3). A fairly uniform floor level occurs in Units 1, 2 and 3 at − 3.74 m.; in Unit 1, topsoil came down onto this floor. Another floor, at − 4.61 m., was found in Units 2 and 3; in the latter unit, layers of red earth fill with many fallen stones occurred above this floor.

The period of use of these buildings has been placed in LC II; the deposit over the building debris dates to LC IIIA.

TRENCH 17—THE ROAD

In a trench 10 m. long and 1.50 m. wide (fig. 13), running east to west and located to the northwest of the threshing floor and about 1.50 m. below it, a road ca. 2.50 m. wide was disclosed. It was constructed with regularly laid curbing in either side, filled behind with loose stones in

earth. The trench was doubled in width across the roadway, and then a series of seven small cuts were made to trace the course of the road. From Trench 17, it began to curve slightly to the northeast; it was traced in this direction for about 30.0 m. South of Trench 17, the road ran roughly southward for about 35.0 m. and then angled slightly to the west, where it was traced for another 10.0 m. Thus, the road has been found in spots over a total length of 75.0 m., running roughly north-south and passing about 10.0 m. west of the well. Its highest point was found in Cut IV. At the various points where the road was disclosed, its width varied from 2.00 m. to 2.50 m., or possibly more. In Cut VIII, a pavement was found to the southwest of the road, possibly indicating the existence of an open square at this point.

TRENCH 18

Just to the west of Cut IV for the road, a trench 20.0 m. long and 1.50 m. wide was opened, running roughly east-west. It yielded no traces of walls, but a *chavara* fill was found everywhere. It was a fill brought in to level off the unevenness of the rock, apparently to form a large open area, or square, close to the road and the great well.

AREA D

Benson 1969, 20-22 (pl. 9a-d)

The excavation of Area D was begun late in the 1938 season and resumed in 1939. The area lies low on the western slope of Bamboula (fig. 1), not far from where the old Paphos-Limassol road leaves the hill and heads towards Episkopi. The surface of the land before excavation sloped gradually from − 9.35 m. in the east to − 9.71 m. in the west. This end of Bamboula is relatively shallow, and the fact that it is easily accessible from the village of Episkopi has made it a favorite field for would-be plunderers. Thus the area has been subject to much disturbance.

The area opened, measuring 12.40 m. x 15.00 m. (fig. 15), contains remains which have been assigned to one large house and parts of one or two others. The first house consists of rooms 1 through 7 (fig. 16); there are remains of a second house to the northwest of the first (fig. 15),

while the remains in the very north corner of the area may have belonged to a third house. None of these houses has been completely excavated. Paved floors were reached and cleared in Rooms 1, 3, 4, 5 and 6, while in Rooms 2 and 7 the lowest levels reached appeared to be secondary floors on accumulation over the original pavements. Room 8 was an open courtyard which was cleared to bedrock in all but the western corner. In the remaining sections, the excavation was carried far enough to reveal the location of the walls, but did not reach occupation levels.

House I (fig. 16) was apparently L-shaped, with one arm of the L formed by Rooms 3 and 4, the other by 1 and 7, and possibly other rooms beyond these. The two arms of the L joined in room 2. The space within the L was filled by a secondary unit composed of Rooms 5 and 6, and possibly another room to the southeast. The plan is comparable to that of Houses A.V and A.VIII, though it occurs here in a more elaborate version.

The house measured at least 9.90 m. by 11.20 m. and had large and fairly regular rooms. The northwest wing contained the chief rooms of the house. The large quantity of storage pottery found in Rooms 1 and 7 indicates that these were storerooms. The central part of Room 6 was enclosed by a coping of small stones (pl. 9a, left) and was raised slightly above the level of the outer part of the floor; both sections were paved with plaster. This may have been a bathroom. A low foundation ran along the inside of the southwest wall of the room; its purpose is not clear but it may have been a bench. It blocked a doorway, however, 1.00 m. wide, which led from the western corner of Room 6 into Room 7, and may have antedated the construction of the house. The doorway is flanked by large rough hewn blocks, approximately rectangular in shape; a row of flat stones lay in front of the doorway in Room 7.

There may have been a doorway connecting the northern corner of Room 6 with Room 5. The wall is destroyed at this point, but one of the two large stone slabs which lie on the floor in the line of the wall may be a threshold block *in situ*. There was probably a doorway from the northern corner of Room 7 into Room 1, and there was one from the northern corner of Room 1 into Room 2. Owing to the poor preservation of the walls, the width and other details of these doorways could not be determined. A doorway 1.00 m. wide led from the eastern corner of Room 2 into Room 3; another, 1.10 m. wide or less, connected the northern corner of Room 3 with Room 4.

The walls of House I vary in width from 0.40 m. to 0.60 m. The surface of the masonry is rougher than that noted in Area A. Corners and doorways, however, were usually built of large rough-hewn rectangular blocks, which show greater care than do comparable parts in Area A. With House I larger than any in Area A, it would be surprising to find its construction inferior. It is possible that the rough surfaces of many of the preserved walls of Area D were concealed by an outer coating, now largely destroyed. Evidence of such a coating was found in Room 4, where large, thin slabs of stone were placed vertically, as orthostates, against the northwestern and southwestern walls of the room (pl. 9b) and similar stones were

found in the debris. In the debris in Room 4 were also found many fragments of plaster with a smooth outer surface, which appear to have fallen from the walls; these indicate the finish of the wall above the orthostates. Wall plaster was found in quantity only in this room; other rooms may have had a clay coating which has not survived.

The doubling of the northeast wall of Room 4 (pl. 9c) was apparently done by the occupant of the house to the northeast of House I. The plaster floor of the room to the northeast of Room 4 runs under the outer wall and up to the inner wall, evidence that the doubling of the wall, probably for reinforcement, was done from the outside of House I.

Plaster floors were found in Rooms 3, 4, 5 and 6. In Rooms 2 and 7 the excavation reached firm floors of clay with an admixture of lime; the latter were probably secondary floors lying over the original paving.

A rectangular stone block stood on its side in the center of Room 3 and was most probably a post support. An undisturbed accumulation 0.07 m. thick was found over the original floor of Room 7 and there was 0.14 m. of accumulation over that of Room 3. Similar accumulation in Rooms 1 and 2 was not excavated. Building debris was encountered immediately below the plowed top soil and went to the accumulation over the floors. This debris was 0.36 m. in Room 1, 0.43 m. in Room 2, 0.35 m. in Room 3, 0.48 m. in Room 4 and 0.41 m. in Room 7; debris to a depth of 0.19 m. was found in the courtyard, Room 8.

House II was only partially explored. Building debris was removed to a point where the tops of the foundations were visible. The walls of House II have approximately the same orientation as those of House I. Too little was exposed to indicate much about the plan of House II.

The most interesting feature of Area D is a large cellar in the northern corner (fig. 17); it is 6.70 m. long, with a maximum breadth of 3.60 m. and a height which averages more than 2.00 m. The cellar was apparently formed by the artificial enlargement of a natural cave, which corresponded approximately to the central part of the cellar. Tunnels on the north and west are man-made; they probably followed soft veins or fissures in the rock. No masonry was used in the construction of the cellar. Its entrance was a small hole in the roof, located close against the southwest wall of the room through which it was entered (pl. 9d). The opening is at one side of the cave, but no attempt was made to cut steps into the cave wall. In all probability, the cellar was entered with the use of a ladder.

There is no question of the cellar having once been a tomb. The entrance to the cave bears no similarity to dromos types of Bronze Age tombs, while the shape of the cellar is not that of a tomb. The location of the cellar in a house, the absence of bones, and the nature of the finds, consisting largely of storage pottery, also speak against its having been a tomb.

The cellar had been entered and disturbed by plunderers. Storage jars and other vases, which must at one time have stood in order, were found broken into pieces and scattered. There was little or no obviously intrusive material, and it was clear

that not much had been removed by the plunderers. The cellar was found filled with a great quantity of broken pottery, a few figurines, some stone implements and whorls, as well as fourteen inscriptions in the Cypro-Minoan syllabary.[1] It is the vast mass of pottery, in particular, which is pertinent for dating the period of use of the cellar and, as Daniel had assumed, the house as well. As analyzed by Benson (1969, 20-21), the pottery indicated that the cellar was in use in the LC IIC period. Some pottery on the floors of House I may be as early, but other accumulation shows continued use into LC IIIA. There is no clear evidence for the exact time of the destruction of the area within LC III.

---

1. Daniel 1941; see especially Appendix I, New Inscriptions from the Bamboula Site, Kourion; Catalogue of Inscriptions, Nos. 1, 2, 8, 9, 24, 28, 40, 58, 62, 72, 73, 75, 81 and 82.

CHAPTER IV

AREA E

AREA E

Benson 1969, 22-28; 1970, 30-35

Area E was dug almost entirely during the 1939 season of excavations, as Trenches 20 and 21. When Daniel returned to Bamboula in 1948, the first work he did was in Area E—cleaning, probing and investigating further. Unfortunately, little of the work of the 1948 season would be incorporated into his text. Benson has already noted how much less satisfactory was the evidence from this area than was that from Area A (Benson 1969, 22). Benson himself conducted a brief excavation in 1954 to "gain some firsthand knowledge of the nature and problems of Area E." (*loc. cit.*). My own work in 1951 concentrated on this area, for it was the one which posed the greatest problems and for which Daniel's notes gave the least satisfactory guidance. The result, as mentioned in the Introduction, was the use of Daniel's text only for details; the text given here is entirely new and the interpretation of the house plans in many cases quite different from that of Daniel. This has involved a new numbering of the houses, which was already seen necessary by Benson and which results from the reinterpretation of Daniel's House I as two separate houses, giving a total of eight rather than seven houses in Area E.

Area E (fig. 1) is located on the northwest side of Bamboula, on its lower slopes and along the edge of the rock shelf (pl. 9e), under which lay a number of the Late Bronze Age tombs at Bamboula (Benson 1972, 3). The total length of the area is 70.0 m., while its width varied from as little as 3.0 m. from the present cliff face, which has receded greatly in places through the millennia, to as much as 30.0 m. at its southwest end, including the extension here dug by Benson in 1954; it is 18.50 m. wide at its northeast end. The rock ledge is highest in the northeastern part of the area and here, where Houses I and II were built, the fill was very shallow, and almost no construction remains above the rock surface, although some floors are preserved (Frontispiece). On the line between Houses II and III, the rock was cut down for 0.70 to 0.80 m., resulting in much better preservation of the walls of both House III and those that were later built over it. The rock rises to its natural surface for the width of the Street of the Tombs, between Houses III and IV, but it is again cut down southwest of the street, and the two houses in the southwest part of the area thus offer better preserved masonry. In the southern corner of the area, the rock ledge drops suddenly and here there is considerable depth of deposit and some pre-house remains.

The interrelationship of houses and tombs in Area E is a matter of considerable architectural interest. Many tombs were cut in the northwest face of the cliff and were entered from outside and below the level on which the houses were founded. Other tombs were entered from the Street of the Tombs, between Houses III and IV (fig. 25), while still others lay to the southeast of the block of Houses I-III, where another street is postulated, as well as beyond House I to the northeast, where there would have been a street parallel to the Street of the Tombs. Still farther to the northeast beyond this street the bulk of the tombs is located. While tombs lay beneath most of the houses, the entrance to these tombs seems always to have been from outside the area of the houses themselves. The tomb entrances, other than those from the cliff side, thus seem to be a good guide to the network of streets, on the one hand, or for delineation of areas where there was no housing.

HOUSE E.I (pl. 10a-b)
Benson 1969, 22-23; A:2, A:3, A:5, A:9, A:10 and B:2

Benson's analysis of the stratigraphy of the area has shown quite clearly that House I was the first to be built in Area E, that it was constructed in the LC IA period and was in use throughout LC IIA and B; after remodeling as House VII, it was in use in LC IIIA.

The plan of House I (fig. 18), derived very largely from a study of cuttings in rock (see fig. 25), shows the same three long units, each of which is composed of a long and a short room, as has already been noted in House A.VI (see above, pp. 20-22). As is the case there, and in some of the other houses of this type in Area E, the long room may be divided, usually into two rooms of roughly equal size. A unique feature of House I is the small addition to the exterior in the form of what must have been a shed opening onto the street along the northeast side of the house.

Very little remains of masonry still resting on the shelves cut into the rock for the walls. There is a small piece between the entrance hall, Room 1, and the shed, Room 8; another piece of the same size remains in the central wall in Room 1, still another bit on the wall between Rooms 6 and 7, and the only piece which gives the full width of a wall between Rooms 3 and 6. These inner walls averaged 0.70 to 0.80 m. in width, and the same width holds for the exterior wall of Room 1, to which the shed is attached. We have taken 0.75 m. as a standard wall width, except for the party

wall of Houses I-II, which must have been about 1.10 m. wide. The only exterior wall of which any part is preserved is that between Room 1 and the shed; the cutting for the party wall is very clear. The location of the southeast wall of the house is determined without any doubt by the southeast edge of the floor of Room E.1.4; the wall has been given the standard width and has been extended on this line for the full length of the house, as well as of the other two in the same block, Houses II and III. The evidence for the location of the cliff wall, on the northwest side of the house, is less satisfactory; its position is most closely determined by the rock cutting which gives one side of the doorway from Room 5 to Room 6; the doorway has been given a width of 1.00 m., which seems to have been fairly standard in these houses, and the wall has been given the usual width. This line has then been extended parallel with the southeast wall for the full length of the block. Nowhere else in the block is there any indication of the correctness of this line of wall, though the pit in House II.5 indicates that the line cannot be placed farther to the southeast.

The entrance to House I is from the street at the northeast through a doorway 1.15 m. wide, with a small post hole that centers on the northeast wall of Room 2, the outer face of which is aligned with the inner face of the wall between Room 1 and the shed. From Room 1 to Room 2 there is a doorway 1.80 m. wide which has a larger posthole at its center. Down the center of Room 1 is a wall ca. 0.60 m. thick that runs for 1.50 m., leaving 1.00 m. on either side of the wall and the same distance between the end of the wall and that between 1 and 7. The most logical architectural explanation for this wall is that it helped support a stairway to the second storey. Either or both post holes may have helped support the upper part of the stairway and/or a landing in the second storey. Room 1 had an earth floor over the rock at − 6.65 m.

Rooms 2 and 3 together most probably formed a large L-shaped courtyard. Most of the area of Room 2 was heavily damaged by the plow, as was the southeastern half of Room 3. Debris of the LC III reoccupation of the house came down onto the court floor at − 6.83 m.; beneath this was a floor of *chavara* plaster. The deposit below the floor, from − 6.87 to − 7.07 m., dates to LC IIA

(Benson 1969, A:9). A pit with deposit of the LC IB phase (Benson 1969, A:5) is at the center of the northwestern half of Room 3, while the pit against the wall between 3 and 1 is of the LC IIB phase (Benson 1969, B:2). A large number of postholes are scattered throughout the well-preserved half of Room 3 (fig. 25), indicating the existence of a light structure, or structures, in the court. A few of these are in a position to have helped support a balcony over the northwestern half of Room 3, which most likely continued over Room 1 as well.

Room 4 is much the most satisfactorily preserved part of House I, thanks to the pavement of large pebbles which clearly outlines the position of three walls of the room (pl. 10a); a later cutting destroyed the northwestern end of the room. A second pavement, of smaller pebbles, lay above the first at −6.63 m. and both of these pavements continued under the later wall that was added for the remodelled second use of House I, as House VII. The rock ledge for the walls on the three sides of the room that are preserved is ca. 0.10-0.20 m. above the large pebble pavement (pl. 10b). These rock ledges are denuded and thus give no indication of the position of doorways; the door to Room 3 was most probably near the northwestern end of the room and the door to Room 5 in the northwest end wall.

These is no evidence for Room 5 in the original house since it was completely destroyed by the deeper cutting for the reconstruction. That it existed is clearly indicated by the doorway to Room 6, which has an LC I wall and floor. Although the cutting for the wide party wall along the southwest side of Room 5 was altered during the reconstruction, its earlier existence seems clear. The LC III debris of House VII went right down onto the rock in the area of Room 5.

Room 6 still retains two bits of LC I wall on the rock-cut shelves on its southeast and northeast sides. Its earliest plaster floor, at −7.08 m., stops at these walls and gives the limits of the room to the southwest as well. Doorways to Rooms 3 and 7, which most probably existed, must remain hypothetical, though that to Room 3 must have been between the two remaining pieces of masonry and, since doorways in these houses are almost always at or near the corners of rooms, the door to Room 7 was most likely aligned with that to Room 5.

The floor of Room 6 at −7.08 m. was covered with LC IA debris (Benson 1969, A:3), indicating the dates for the early use of the house.

The leveling of the rock for the southeast wall of Room 7 during the early period seems clear and continued the line of the wall between Rooms 3 and 6. There is no indication of the line of the northeast wall of Room 7, which here is shown as a continuation of the line of that of Room 1. The earliest floor of the room is at −6.79 m. and is of plaster; a second floor was at −6.65 m. and on it was found LC II debris.

The lean-to against the northeast wall of House I, Room 8, was most likely of light construction, supported by a line of posts for which six postholes are preserved. The southeast end of the lean-to seems to have been closed by a short wall running into the street from the entrance to Room 1.

Despite the scant nature of the building remains of House I, the plan which it has been possible to reconstruct is that of a known type of Late Cypriote house, well documented in House A.VI. Both have the tripartite arrangement—three long sections, each further divided into a long room and a short one; the center large room is the courtyard. In each case, there is good evidence that there was a second storey over the small rooms, though the stairways to the upper storey are different in E.I and A.VI. It is also highly likely that the stairway led to a long balcony in front of the three upper rooms, which would have given access to them and would, at the same time, have sheltered part of the courtyard. Where the two houses differ most is in size: E.I is more than half again as large as A.VI; interior dimensions of E.I come to some 110 square meters, while those for A.VI are only about 65 square meters. This exceptional size for E.I is characteristic of most of the other houses of Area E.

The latest accumulation on the floors of House I is of the LC IIB phase (Benson 1969, B:2) and this is of the period of use. There is no building debris of this first phase of the house, for it was reconstructed and enlarged as House VII in LC IIIA.

HOUSE E.II (pl. 10c)
Benson 1969, 23; A:4, A:6, A:7 and A:8

As in House I, the earliest accumulation over

any of the floors of House II is of the LC IA phase (Benson 1969, A:4), and Benson has suggested that the two houses were contemporaneous. From architectural considerations, principally the wide party wall common to the two houses, their contemporaneity is obvious.

House II (fig. 18) is situated slightly lower on the rock terrace than House I. The rock has been cut down artificially along the southwest side of the party wall, the cutting varying in height from 0.37 m. at the southeast end (pl. 10c) to almost nothing at the northwest; the mean height, at the center, is 0.25 m. In the area of House II, the rock shelf slopes down gently from southeast to northwest. Under the southeast wall of Room 2, the rock falls away suddenly, as it does in many places on the terrace, and here the depression is ca. 0.45 m. deep; how far it extends to the southwest is not known since there is an unexcavated stretch, but where the excavation again reveals the southeast wall and street, in front of House III.3, the rock is again at the higher level. Thus the southeast wall of II.2 required a deep foundation, and the narrow space between the foundation and the rock was filled by a packing of stones, large sherds and earth as a foundation for the floor of Room 2. All the other walls of House II were founded on rock, but only one small bit of masonry remains of the wall between Rooms 1 and 6, and this was partly embedded in one of the later walls of House VII, which took over part of House II as well as House I.

Room 1 is clearly delimited along its northeast side by the cutting down of the rock on the southwest face of the party wall (pl. 10c). The scrap of masonry locates its northwest wall, while the finished southwest edge of this wall indicates the position of the doorway from Room 1 to Room 6. Such a central position for a doorway is unusual at Bamboula, but two doorpost stones on the side of Room 6 confirm that the door was here; it was probably 1.20 m. wide. Both the southwest and southeast walls of Room 1 have been assumed to be extensions of walls of Room 6 and Room 2, but there is no other evidence for their position. There are remains of a floor at −7.25 m., with which goes a pit that contained LC IIA remains (Benson 1969, A:8). The large LC I pit was below this floor.

There is almost no record of the excavation in

the area of Room 2. Its southeast wall is located by the packing for the floor between the rock face and the wall foundation. Its southwest wall's location depends on the rock cutting on the side of Room 3, while the only indication of the possible location of the northwest wall comes from the doorpost on the southwest side of the door from Room 2 to Room 5. Running down the length of the room, a little to the southwest of its center, is a line of four postholes, with flat stones between, most probably from a light structure in the courtyard. The entrance to the courtyard must have been from the street to the southeast. In the northeastern half of the room is a carefully built pit with small channels on either side running into it.

The long, narrow Room 3 has its northeast, northwest and southwest walls clearly located by rock cuttings. Nothing else is known of the features of this area. Room 4 is of the same width and even longer, assuming that its northeast wall is an extension of that of Room 3, which seems to be assured by the location of the doorpost between Rooms 2 and 5. Little can be said of this area, except that a high percentage of LC I sherds were found here and in the southwestern part of Room 5. The great, square Room 5 is, unfortunately, little known. Over it lay part of the later house, at a different orientation, that occupied much of the area of both Houses II and III. There is evidence for a *chavara* floor that belonged to II.5, while the pit in the northern corner of the room may also have been dug in this earlier phase.

It is Room 6 which offers the most important stratigraphic indications for House II. A *chavara* floor, sometimes mixed with clay, at −7.46 m. stops short of the location of the wall between Rooms 1 and 6 shown on the plan (fig. 18), indicating that the wall originally was a little farther to the northwest, perhaps in line with the wall from 2 to 5. A little higher, at −7.42 m., there is another *chavara* floor, while at −7.30 m. there is a floor of very firm clay. Although there were no sherds on the two lower floors, there were LC IA sherds on the floor at −7.30 m. (Benson 1969, A:4). A fourth floor, at −7.25 m., had LC IIA sherds on it (Benson 1969, A:6). The well in the eastern corner of Room 6, 5.00 m. deep, had LC IIA sherds from the period of use at its bottom (Benson 1969, A:7); it may have been dug as early as LC I. It was closed by an LC III wall from the later house over House II.

Like House I, House II would seem to have been abandoned in LC IIB. While House I was incorporated into the large House VII of the LC III period, House II was succeeded by a house with a different orientation, which was also of the LC III period, as well as by the enlargement of House VII. House II was even larger than House I, over 140 square meters as against 110 square meters for House I. Except for Rooms 3 and 4, its rooms were unusually large. While the plan retains the tripartite divisions, each division is subdivided approximately in half, rather than into long and short rooms, a scheme used again in both Houses III and IV. This new plan may be accounted for by the fact that none of these three houses has given any evidence of a second storey, for it was most probably the stairway and the balcony which determined the small size of the second-storey rooms and, in turn, those beneath them. The very large area of House II may also have alleviated the necessity for a second storey, and it then set the pattern for Houses III and IV, both built subsequent to II.

HOUSE E.III (pl. 10d)
Benson 1969, 23-24; B:1, C:1

Both the stratigraphy and architectural considerations indicate clearly that House III was built later than Houses I and II. Whereas the southwest wall of House II had rested on a rock cutting just a bit above the floors of Rooms 3 and 4, this wall must have been reconstructed when it became the party wall for Houses II and III. The rock ledge seems then to have been cut back for almost its entire width, and for a depth of ca. 0.80 m. in the northeast sides of III.2 and 8, about 0.70 m. in Room 1; later disturbance in Room 7 makes it impossible to determine the depth of the cutting there, but it must have continued much the same as in Room 8. The foundations of the party wall were then built from the bottom of this cutting. Such a deep cutting was apparently necessitated by the desire to level off a natural depression in the rock in the area of House III. When the rock was leveled in this area, the cuttings along the southwest side of Room E.III.4 were 0.30 to 0.40 m. deep. The greatest depth, in the southern corner of Room E.III.5,

was ca. 0.50 m.; then the rock of the street sloped down to the northwest and at the cliff was about level with the area cleared for House III. Along the southeast side of the house, and at a point where a bit of masonry from the outer wall of Room 3 is preserved, the depth of the cutting was ca. 0.70 m.; to the northeast, for the rest of the width of Room 3 and the length of Room 2, the area is unexcavated. The limits of the house on the northwest side, above the cliff, may have been marked by a few stones which were left here after the 1939 excavations but have since been removed. It is in the width of House III that the cliff is preserved farthest to the northwest (see fig. 25). That the line used for the northwest walls of all three houses in this block is approximately correct may be indicated by the fact that it makes the two halves of House III about equal in width, as indicated in the length of Rooms 3 and 6.

One exceptional feature in the overall plan of House III is the cutting off of its southern corner. While the Street of the Tombs and the street along the southeast side of Houses I-III might have met at a right angle, the width of the street was increased by cutting the corner at about a 45 degree angle (see pl. 10d, upper left); this is well marked by the deep rock cutting. The pre-existence of Tombs 19 and 34, which are of LC II date (Benson 1972, 22-23, 29), may have been responsible for the widening of the streets at the corner.

House III is the primary representative of the LC IIB period at Bamboula, though its use continued into LC IIC (Benson 1969, 23-24; B:1, C:1). In the following period, LC IIIA, the area of House III was occupied in part by some of House V and in part by House VI. It was the deep digging for the floor of House VI which destroyed much of the northwestern half of House III. The depth of the cutting into the rock for House III, however, has meant that a number of stretches of wall in the northeastern part of the house were preserved; House V, built over this part of House III, was at the higher level of House II. These walls average 0.60 m. in width, less than those in Houses I and II, and they are fairly well built of somewhat squared stones.

The best-preserved room in House III is Room 1 (pl. 10d); its walls are in place on three sides, while the fourth side has the deep cutting for the party wall. Walls between 1 and 2, and 1 and 8, abutted on the party wall. The cross wall between 1 and 3 is at right angles to these walls, forming a rectangular room. The straight, southeast end of this wall indicates that there was a doorway here, 1.10 m. wide. A pot was found in the southeast side of the doorway. The floor of the room was divided into two parts, with a large raised platform in the eastern corner, which had a border of stones and was paved with stone chips; the rest of the floor, at − 8.23 m., was paved with potsherds. A pithos in the western corner of the room had its mouth flush with the sherd floor. This floor was cut by the footing trenches for the house built above it. The accumulation over the floor was of LC IIB date, but above this the area was filled up to the level of the rock ledge for House II with LC IIIA debris in preparation for the building of House V.

Very little of the area of Room 2 was excavated, but a plaster floor at − 8.12 m. was found to run continuously into Room 3, indicating where the doorway was located and suggesting the symmetrical arrangement shown in the restored plan (fig. 18). A good part of this plaster floor was preserved over much of Room 3, and the edge of the floor gave the position of the wall to Room 6. Above this floor, at − 8.12 m., there were several floors, often of *chavara,* up to − 8.06 m. Above this was LC IIB fill to − 7.91 m. and then the deep LC IIIA fill.

The areas of both Rooms 4 and 5 were badly disturbed by later construction. There are cuttings in the rock which give the position of the northeast and southwest walls of Room 4, but the wall between 4 and 5 is not documented and has been drawn to be continuous with that between 1 and 8, and 3 and 6. At the center of Room 5 there is a section of original LC II fill with floors at − 8.66 m., − 8.63 m. and − 8.58 m., while the fill rises to − 8.28 m. The wall between 5 and 6 most probably stopped just short of the LC IIB-C bothros. It is here suggested that the entrance to House III may have been in the western corner of Room 5, from the Street of the Tombs; it would then have given entrance into an L-shaped courtyard, similar to that in House I. Here street and house were at the same level. While an entrance to the house into Room 3 cannot be precluded, and it would fit the pattern of House E.II and

House A.VI, the floor of 3 was below the street level to the southeast and would have required some construction; there is space either side of the preserved bit of masonry in the wall of 3 for such a doorway. The entrance into Room 5 is probably to be preferred, and an argument in its favor is the existence of an entrance from the street in just this position in the succeeding house. This too led into an L-shaped courtyard, most of which was over III.6. A *chavara* floor at − 8.38 m. in III.6 was most probably the court floor, which was then re-used in the court of the later house.

The areas of Rooms 7 and 8 are again badly disturbed, with no floors preserved in the former area. An earlier wall between 7 and 8, indicated by dotted lines, has a floor at − 8.18 m. which goes up to it; the floor at − 8.14 m., on the other hand, probably belongs to the time when this wall was out of use and the wall between 7 and 8 was relocated; we have used the line of the short spur off the wall between 5 and 6 for the line of the new wall between 7 and 8. With doorways as shown, it would give another pair of rooms very similar to 1 and 2.

House III is thus another rectangular house which shows the tripartite divisions and which, like House II, has three long sections subdivided about in half. The house has inner dimensions very close to those of House I, with a total area of about 110 square meters. It is the further division of each half of the northeasternmost section, giving a series of four rooms in the depth of the house, which differentiates it from both Houses I and II.

THE STREET OF THE TOMBS (pl. 11a)

To the southwest of House III is the Street of the Tombs, 4.20 m. wide and clearly delimited on both sides by cuttings for the adjacent houses (pl. 11a). The highest point of the street is over Tomb 5; it slopes down both to the northwest and the southeast. Tomb 5 was centered under the street, while Tomb 34, to the southeast, was a little farther to the southwest side of the street. The street most probably continued to the southeast, where Tomb 33 would have been under it. The rock of the street, very close to the surface, was denuded of any pavements that might have been laid over it. In the LC IIIA period, the street was narrowed at its northwestern end where House VI intruded into it (fig. 25).

HOUSE E.IV (pl. 11b-d)
Benson's House VI; Benson 1969, 25-27;
D:1d, D:2b

Although separated from the block formed by Houses I-III by the Street of the Tombs, House IV seems architecturally to be part of the same series and would logically have been built after House III, that is, not earlier than LC IIB. Its walls are parallel to those of House III; its median walls northeast-southwest follow the same line as those of House III; it has the same tripartite plan, with long sections subdivided approximately in half by cross walls; what slight evidence there is for its southeast wall suggests that it continues the line of the southeast side of the block formed by Houses I-III. The northwest wall, on the other hand, has been drawn in about 0.80 m., just the width of the northwest wall of the block; this was probably dictated by the face of the cliff in this area.

This departure from Benson's stratigraphic sequence, done here for architectural reasons, can be justified. Actually, Benson (1969, 25) has already stated, "that the floors of House VI were not cut through. Thus, there is no sherd evidence available for the existence of the house before the LC IIIA period. Although an additional investigation in the 1948 campaign seems to indicate that it did not exist before the LC IIIA period, there are nevertheless cogent architectural reasons for postulating the existence of a house in this position at a much earlier date." What the architectural evidence given above does suggest is that House IV (Benson's House VI) was planned and built here before House VI (Benson's House IV) —of the same tripartite plan but with a different orientation—was constructed over Houses II and III. The evidence for the date of House VI will be given more fully in the proper place, but just to summarize it here, it indicates that House VI was built and first occupied toward the end of the LC IIC period. This should give a *terminus ante quem* for the construction of House IV, which cannot then have been built earlier than LC IIB, when House III was constructed, and not later than LC IIC, when House VI was built.

Little enough remains of House IV (fig. 19): a

large part of Rooms 1 and 2 remains unexcavated; all of Room 6 and half of Rooms 5 and 7 have been taken away by quarrying operations and the consequent recession of the cliff face. What remains, however, offers many points of interest. Each of the three divisions of House IV—alone among the houses of this type—is 4.20 m. wide, the same width as the Street of the Tombs. It is thus the largest of any of these houses, with an interior area that must have been about 150 square meters. Whether or not the width of the street was taken as a unit can only be surmised, but it would seem to be more than coincidence that the divisions of the house have the same width. The use of such a unit, however, does indicate that there was nothing to restrict the extent of the house from northeast to southwest.

In general, the rock in the area of House IV was trimmed to a level ca. 0.30 m. lower than in House III, resulting in the preservation of more masonry in House IV than in any of the earlier houses in the block to the northeast. The walls average 0.60 m. in width, as in House III. There are long stretches of masonry on both the northeast and southwest outer walls of the house, as well as rock cuttings which help to make the position of these walls precise. As remarked above, the recession of the cliff face has destroyed all of the northwest outer wall except the very southwest corner, where there is a cutting in the rock for the inner corner. The position of the northwest outer wall at this point is confirmed by the fact that the extension of the line of the northwest outer wall of House VIII, given by a considerable stretch of its masonry, brings it exactly to this point. The line of the northwest outer wall of House IV has been made parallel with the cross walls between Rooms 1 and 7, and 2 and 6. Most of the southeast outer wall still lies unexcavated, but where it is exposed, on the southeast side of Room 3, and where a long stretch of masonry is preserved, the line of the wall is slightly oblique, rather than parallel to the northwest wall of Room 3. Rather than continue this line across the house, which would make Rooms 1 and 2 trapezoidal, and Room 3 as well, we have chosen to straighten out the line so that it continues the line of the southeast outer walls of Houses I-III; only excavation can ascertain the actual line of the wall.

More than half of Room 1 remains undug, but

the part that has been excavated has some interesting features. There is masonry for the full length of the excavated part of the northeast outer wall; the rock cuttings for the base of the wall between 1 and 7 are clear right across the room, and some of the masonry is preserved for three courses, to a height of 0.40 m.; the cuttings for the base of the wall between 1 and 2 are also distinct right up to the undug section. Against this last wall lies a rock platform, ca. 0.15 m. high, along the northeastern edge of which is a hole into which a vase was probably set. From the northwest side of 1, there was an entrance to a great cavelike room, probably a stable, most under Rooms 1 and 2. No indications of a doorway, or doorways, were found in the exposed walls of Room 1. The rock in the area of Room 1 is at −8.81 m. and a floor was found at −8.77 m.; two pits were cut through this floor; above the floor were found first undisturbed accumulation of LC IIIA date and then building debris of the same date (Benson 1969, D:1d and D:2b).

Almost two-thirds of Room 2 remains unexcavated. We have already noted the well-marked rock cuttings for the wall between 1 and 2; on the side of 2 this cutting may be 0.30 to 0.40 m. high. The rock cuttings for the wall between 2 and 6 are equally definite and vary from 0.10-0.20 m. on the side of room 2 (pl. 11c, right side). The rock cutting for the base of the wall between 2 and 4 is clear only on the side of 2 (pl. 11b, upper center). The wide doorway from 2 to 6, about 1.30 m., is clearly delineated in rock cuttings, but no doorway to either 1 or 4 is marked. The rock floor of room 2 is at −8.62 m. and on it rests building debris. In the western part of the room, there is a slightly raised section which is bordered by small stones and lined with plaster; it runs off to the northeast to a pot sunk into the floor (pl. 11c).

As in the northeastern of the three long divisions of House III, the southwestern long division of House IV is not only subdivided approximately in half, but the southeastern half of it is then divided further into two rooms, 3 and 4. Of these, 3 is almost twice as large as 4 (pl. 11d). We have already noted that the southeast outer wall of Room 3 is slightly oblique to its northwest inner wall; masonry is preserved for almost the whole length of both of these walls, the reason being that

Room 3 rests on fill in a large depression in the rock, as does much of the southeastern part of House VIII. The street wall has a foundation wider than the wall; it is rather shallow and rests on fill, and the line of the foundation is not quite parallel with that of the wall. The wall itself is preserved for a height of ca. 0.30 m.; it ends at a doorway and the greater width of the foundation at this point is used as a step down to the street. The southwest wall of Room 3, which was part of the outer wall until it became the party wall with House VIII, has its masonry preserved for three courses, a height of 0.40 m. The wall between Rooms 3 and 4 is founded on a rock ledge; it has a stretch of masonry preserved, which at the southwest ends at a doorway in the same position and of the same width as the street door. On the side of Room 3, the rock ledge for the wall between it and Room 4 has a height of 0.40 m. at the door and 0.70 m. at the northern corner of the room. The lower floor of Room 3 is at −8.99 m., above which was found the same type of deposit as in Room 1.

Room 4 is barely more than 2.00 m. wide and somewhat over twice as long. There are clear rock cuttings for its southwest wall and much of its southeast wall; its wall with Room 5 is marked by a clear cutting on the side of 5 and, as we have seen, the wall with Room 2 is set by a rock cutting on the side of 2. It may be assumed that there was a doorway between 4 and 5, corresponding to that between 3 and 4. The rock floor varies from 0 to 0.10 m. higher than that in Room 2, while at a point just to the northeast of the door between 3 and 4 there is a cutting in the rock, about 0.10 m. high, running right across Room 4. No floor levels are mentioned for this room. The rock cutting across the room, as well as the narrowness of the room, suggest the possibility that there was a staircase to a second storey in Room 4, though no trace of its structure has been noted. May this not have been true in III.1 as well?

While the northern half of Room 5 is gone, the southern half is clearly outlined by rock cuttings on both its southeast and southwest sides; a long stretch of masonry remains on the latter. The rock cuttings for the wall between Rooms 4 and 5 is 0.17 m. deep at the door, 0.28 m. at the east corner. We have already mentioned that a corner in the rock cutting at the west most probably gives the line of the northwest wall of Room 5, and of the house. The small rectangular cutting shown as an intrusion at the western angle of the room (fig. 25), may have been for a large post built into the wall. Room 5 had a *chavara* floor at −8.95 m., which was burned black by the debris which fell on it; above this is building debris of LC IIIA, then a layer up to −8.70 m. with mud brick and clear signs of burning, and finally topsoil. Similar signs of burning occurred in the fill in Room 4, though none is mentioned for Room 3. Although the fire seems to have been localized, it may have resulted in the abandonment of the house; there are no obvious signs of repair or remodeling.

Nothing remains of Room 6 except the wall and doorway shared with Room 2. Room 7, on the other hand, is about half preserved and has clearly marked rock cuttings for its southeast and southwest walls. The cutting for the wall with Room 1 varies in height from 0.15-0.25 m. There is masonry on some of the southeast wall, and there is also a stub wall of masonry preserved in the line of the northeast wall of Room 7; it has a straight edge which indicates a doorway at this point, possibly the main entrance to House IV from the Street of the Tombs. We have noted already the doorway from Room 3 to the outside, but this may have been connected with the Hearth Area that existed just to the south before House VIII was built; it will be discussed in connection with that house. Room 7 had a bedrock floor at −8.97 m. in which were cut many large and small pits; very little earth was found above this floor.

House IV seems definitely to have been the end of the series of four large, rectangular houses built in order from northeast to southwest, all with clearly related plans. A building was later constructed to the southwest of House IV, but Benson has called this House VIII and has given good reason to believe that it was the latest one built in Area E (Benson 1969, 25-28), putting out of use the Hearth Area already mentioned.

HOUSE E.V (pls. 11e; 12a-b)
Benson's House IV; Benson 1969, 24-26;
C:2, C:3 and D:1a

House V is most closely related in plan to Houses I to IV, apparently a large rectangular house with tripartite division, but it was built with a quite different orientation over the remains of Houses II and III, the former of which was abandoned by LC IIB and the latter in LC IIC. The construction and early stage of occupation of House V were still within the LC IIC phase (Benson 1969, C:2 and C:3), but the date of the removal of stones from wall trenches of House V, possibly for the renovation of House VI, and the collapse of V is very early in LC IIIA (Benson 1969, D:1a). Thus, House V had a very short life before its collapse.

The most marked feature of House V is its very different orientation from the previous Houses II and III, over which it was built (fig. 20); the angle between the walls of the later and earlier houses is ca. 30 degrees. Its breadth, inside the northeast and southwest outer walls, is ca. 15.00 m., even greater than that of House IV. This is assuming that Rooms 3 and 4 were originally part of this house, though they may later have become part of House VII, after the collapse of V. Since House V spanned most of the width of House II and two-thirds of that of House III, its walls were founded at two quite different levels, for the rock was cut down ca. 0.70 to 0.80 m. along the southwest side of the party wall of II-III before the latter was built. In the higher area of House II, no masonry from House V is preserved, whereas there are several long stretches of masonry over the lower area where House III had been. It would seem that after the destruction of House III, its area was filled to within ca. 0.20 m. of the higher level of the rock in the area of House II; all this fill is of LC II date. The foundation trenches for the southwestern part of House V were then cut into this fill, and after the foundations were built an ashy leveling layer brought the fill up to the higher rock level. All the masonry would seem to belong to foundations, for it is of a rough character which indicates that it was not meant to be seen. Most of the floors of House V were too close to the surface to be preserved.

Room 1, in the west corner of House V, lying entirely over the deep fill, has masonry preserved for the full length of its north and east sides, but only short stretches on the west and south. A bit of the east side of the room is still undug. The east wall of the room apparently ran uninterrupted through this undug part; the wall to the north of it, however, is wider than that to the south, suggesting the possibility of a doorway between the two unequal parts. The wall is preserved for heights varying from 0.60 to 0.75 m. The south foundation is preserved for ca. 1.50 m., after which the wall trench can be followed for another 2.50 m., though not to the west corner of the room; the height of the masonry at its western end is 0.80 m. Only a bit of the west wall remains at its north end, but its line seems surely to be indicated by the east wall of VI.5, which was built along its exterior. The foundation for the north wall of Room V.1, preserved for 3.00 m. and for a height of as much as 0.55 m., ends in a straight edge, indicating a doorway between it and the east wall leading into Room 2. Clearly, the foundation was not extended for the width of the doorway as well, to support a threshold; either there was no threshold or it was laid on fill. The large pit in the south corner of Room 1 is oriented with its walls and seems surely to belong with this room. In the center of the room were found two stones, one above the other, to serve as a post support (pl. 11e). Over the fill in this room, and probably in a bedding for a floor, was found LC IIC material, which must belong to the initial stage of House V.

Room 2 was founded on fill in its western half, on rock in the east. Whether or not it was all one room cannot now be determined; it would have been exceptionally large. Any trace of a division of the room is gone, if it ever existed. As it is, it is not rectangular, but rather a parallelogram with 98-degree and 82-degree angles. We have already seen its common wall with Room 1 and the bit of its east wall, which continues the line of that of Room 1. There is a short stretch of masonry in the line of its west wall, the rest of the length of which is clearly marked by the rock cuttings for the east side of VI.7 and 8. For its north wall, only the cutting on the side of Room 3 gives its direction, which is parallel with the wall between Rooms 1 and 2. In the southwestern half of this room is the same LC II fill as in Room 1, but no floor is preserved.

There is very little preserved of Room 3, in the northern corner of House V. The clearest wall line, on the east, is given by the rock cutting, which varies from 0.02 m. on the north to 0.19 m. on the south (pl. 12a). This cutting then turns at

right angles to the west at both ends, giving the direction of the north and south walls. There is nowhere any indication of the thickness of these walls. Also, neither the direction nor the thickness of the west wall of Room 3 is given; the room has been made a rectangle, but it is not impossible that the cliff wall continued the line of the northwest walls of Houses VI and VII, which would have made this room a trapezoid. This does not seem highly likely, especially since House VI was not yet built and the generally rectangular shape of House V would most probably have been kept.

The direction of the north and south walls of Room 4 is given by the rather well preserved floor of the room, which is composed of large, flat sea pebbles in the western part and large sherds in the east (pl. 12b). The latter apparently originally covered over a large cavelike opening under the eastern half of the room. The south edge of the floor is preserved for over 2.00 m., the parallel northern edge for a shorter distance, but here a little masonry is also preserved. There is a bit of the western edge, parallel with the rock cutting on the side of Room 3. It seems clear that the floor must originally have been all of pebbles, but when the hollow beneath collapsed, the area was filled in and the floor then laid with sherds. There is no firm idea where the east edge of the room was, but the extension of the sherd floor would indicate that the room went at least as far as here indicated. It, too, was a parallelogram, just like Room 2. There was LC IIC material both under and on the floor in Room 4 (Benson 1969, C:2 and C:3), which is the basis for the period of construction and use of House V.

Little indication exists for the rest of House V. The south wall continues to the east of the east wall of Room 1, a sure indication that there was another room here. On the other hand, there is no wall continuing the line of the wall between Rooms 1 and 2, which might only indicate that there was a doorway here between Room 5 and another room in the southeast corner of the house. It would be most logical to assume that we have here another almost rectangular house divided into three parallel sections, each then subdivided into at least two rooms. Room 5 would normally have been the courtyard, opening onto a street on the east, if one still existed in this area, as would seem likely. Though it was a very large house, we know very little of it, and its duration was unusually short.

HOUSE E.VI (pl. 12c-e)
Benson's House V; Benson 1969, 24-27;
C:5, C:6, D:1b, D:1c and D:2a

When House V was built over Houses II and III, a triangular area was left open over the western part of House III. This was apparently quickly occupied by House VI (pl. 12c), which was being built at the very end of LC IIC (Benson 1969, C:5), but which gives evidence of occupation only with the beginning of LC IIIA (Benson 1969, 24). The odd shape of the plot is clearly evident in the plan of the house, but the smallness of the area was alleviated to some extent by building part of the structure over the Street of the Tombs (fig. 20); another small area was added to the house by allowing Room 8 to go a bit over what had been House II. House VI used the west wall of House V for the east wall of its Rooms 5, 7 and 8; it is likely that the old cliff wall of House III was still standing, at least in part, and this was used in the northwest wall of House VI. When House V collapsed, after only a very short life, a new east wall had to be built, at least for Room 5. There are indications in other places of two phases in the life of House VI, the first while House V existed and the second after it had collapsed.

The oddly shaped area south of House V, east of House VI, and limited on the other sides by the Street of the Tombs and the street southeast of House VI, seems to have served as a courtyard for House VI, here called Room 1. While this has remained largely unexcavated, there are two distinct layers of fill; over the debris of the previous house is an ashy layer that appears to belong to the period of the remodeling of House VI after the collapse of House V, while above this is debris of House VI itself. The wall between Rooms 1 and 2 is still preserved in part to a height of 0.75 m., except at the center where it was destroyed by an intrusion; it is possible that at this point, just in the center of the wall, there was a doorway from the courtyard into Room 2.

Room 2 has all four of its walls preserved to considerable heights: wall 1-2 has already been mentioned, being as much as 0.75 m. high; wall 2-5 is preserved for almost 1.00 m. above the floor; wall 2-3 has a maximum height of almost 0.85 m., and the street wall has a similar height. There was possibly a doorway in the west corner of Room 4, leading to the street, but the height from the floor to the street was ca. 0.50 m., for the floor is very deep in this room, being below −8.49 m. In the north corner of Room 2 there is an oven, preserved to a height of ca. 0.80 m., while to the south of it is a pit cut into the rock (pl. 12d). While Room 2 may have had doorways to both the courtyard and the street, there seem not to have been any to either Room 3 or Room 5.

The walls of Room 3 are also preserved almost all around; only in the northern corner has an intrusion destroyed the wall 3-5. Wall 2-3 is 0.85 m. high, wall 3-4 0.50 m., 3-5 0.40 m. and 3-street 0.30 m. This room was filled up to the −8.28 m. level with the debris of House III, through which its walls had been laid, while its own debris filled it to −8.05 m. Thus, its floor would seem to have been ca. 0.20 m. higher than that of Room 2. The finish of the wall 3-4 suggests that there was a doorway to Room 4 in the north corner of Room 3; the northeast side of the doorway was destroyed by the intrusion here.

Room 4 has some of both its southeast and southwest walls preserved, though the wall 4-street is only one course high. There may have been a doorway in the west corner leading in from the street, which slopes down to the level of the floor of Room 4 at this point. The position of the northwest wall of Room 4, the cliff wall, is marked by the brick bin in the north corner, next to which is a rock cutting for the short northeast wall 4-5, leaving a doorway into 5. A *chavara* plaster floor at −8.64 m. has a pithos in it at the south corner, as well as the bin in the north corner. The floor was covered with the debris of House VI.

Much the largest room in House VI is Room 5, which goes the full width of the house from east to west. Its south wall, with Rooms 2 and 3, we have seen to be preserved almost to 1.00 m. in height. On the other side, the wall with Rooms 6 and 7 is about 0.70 m. high. The wall built to the east, after the collapse of House V, has a height of ca. 0.60 m. There may well have been doorways from 5 to both 6 and 7, in places where there are now gaps in the wall; that to Room 7 seems assured by the finished end of the stub wall in the east corner. The main floor of the room was at −8.38 m., was of *chavara* plaster, and had a number of pits cut into it. This floor may also have served the earlier House III, to which some of the pits may have belonged, and was then cleaned off and used again for House VI. The LC III debris of House VI rested on this floor. In House VI, as in House III, this may have been a courtyard, entered through Room 4, the two forming an L-shaped courtyard as in the previous house.

Like all of the rooms of House VI, 6 and 7 are trapezoidal, but more extremely so as the point of the triangular plot is reached. The wall between 6 and 7 is preserved for its full length to a height of ca. 0.65 m. (pl. 12e). Originally there was a door at the south end of this wall, which was later walled up. Parts of both the north and south walls are preserved; in the south wall, between Rooms 5 and 6, there is space for a doorway at the west end, but there is not space for a doorway between Rooms 6 and 8. Again, the cliff wall is entirely gone. There was a floor at −8.20 m. with considerable LC IIIA pottery on it (Benson 1969, D:1c). There was possibly another floor at −8.16 m., above which was the fallen debris from the house.

Walls or rock cuttings define the entire perimeter of Room 7; that on the east was the wall of House V.2 or the rock cutting for it. The walls with Rooms 5 and 6 have already been discussed; there was a doorway in each one. The wall with Room 8, preserved to a height of ca. 0.75 m., is solid. A bit of plaster facing was found on the party wall with House V.2, on the side of Room 7. There was an uneven *chavara* floor at −8.27 m., on which were found LC IIIA sherds. There was possibly another floor at −8.18 m., on which was the destruction debris of the house.

The small, trapezoidal Room 8 has only its south wall preserved, but rock cuttings define clearly both the east and north sides. The cutting on the east side crossed the division between Houses II and III and cut away the ridge separating them at this point; the cutting is ca. 0.45 m. high on the side of Room 8, while the cutting on the north is ca. 0.30 m. deep. As noted, there seems to have been no communication with either Room 6 or 7. There is no floor preserved from this room, though in the northeast half it was probably at the level of the rock.

Because of the shape of the plot on which it was built, this house has an altogether unorthodox plan. Yet, one can perhaps see in it the standard rectangular plan with tripartite division which has been compressed at one side. Because of the size of the house, the courtyard runs its full width. The difference in floor levels, particularly between Rooms 2 and 3, suggests the possibility that the former was a basement room, or perhaps a room separated from the house with its own communication with both the street and the outside courtyard. There is, however, no other indication that the house had a second storey.

HOUSE E.VII (pl. 13a-b)
Benson 1969, 26-27; D:1e, D:1f, D:1h,
D:2c and D:2d

Although Houses II and III went out of use in LC IIB and IIC respectively and were replaced by Houses V and VI, House I seems to have continued in use into LC IIIA. It was apparently during that phase, and while House V still stood, that House I was reconstructed and expanded to include the area over House II that was not used by House V; this enlarged house is called House VII. Certainly, the orientation of House I was kept for all rooms but 1, which was the link with House V. While we know little of the whole eastern part of House VII, it seems that much of the western half of the house kept the old lines; Room 5 in particular is very close to I.7. New walls were built here, as in the other part of House VII. In the southeastern part of the house, a new wall was built just inside I.4 and following the line of the party wall I-II. The same thing happened to the northeast of the old wall between I.3 and 4. The party wall between Houses V and VII was the north wall of V.3-4, which is about 30 degrees off the line of the main southeast-northwest walls of House VII.

Because of the high level of both Houses I and II, over which House VII was built, few of its walls are preserved. There are two stretches of new walls built over House I, each about 3.50 m. long, a piece of about equal length over House II and a short stretch in the north wall of House V. These walls average 0.60 m. in width. Since there was a difference of ca. 0.25 m. in the rock level between Houses I and II, the rock level in the area of House I was cut down to that of

House II for Rooms VII.2 and 3, as well as for the northeast corner of Room 1. Thus, there are clear new wall cuttings in the rock for these rooms.

Much the largest room in the preserved part of House VII is Room 1 as we have restored it. It is a trapezoid with dimensions running from 4.50 to 6.00 m., which would have been too large for unsupported beams in either direction (pl. 13b, foreground). This seems to have been solved by a row of posts supporting a girder; two stone slabs supported the posts, which ran across the room from northeast to southwest, in line with the wall between Rooms 2 and 3. The maximum span would thus have been reduced to about 3.00 m. There is the possibility that the cliff wall did not follow the old line, but ran parallel with the wall between Rooms 1 and 9; this would have left out the pit in the western corner, which we assumed was used in II.5, but which may have been used in this later period as well. The rock ledge for the wall between Rooms 1 and 2 is cut down ca. 0.33 m. on the side of Room 1, but rises ca. 0.20 m. for the width of the doorway between 1 and 2. The wide rock ledge for the party wall of I-II was cut down ca. 0.50 m. to the level of the floor of Room 1. The doorway between Room 1 and what was Room 4 of House V is also clear, with the door swinging in a quarter-circle cutting in the rock. The floor of the room, at − 7.17 m., was of *chavara* plaster, badly burned by the debris of the house, which fell on it. This floor was littered with pottery and other objects when the house was destroyed by fire: B401, 414, 575, 1251 and 1603. A large pit near the center of the room (pl. 13b) contained a pithos which was removed by Makrides many years ago and is in the Cyprus Museum.

Room 2 is very small and trapezoidal, with its northeast wall preserved and the other three clearly marked by rock cuttings (pl. 13a, upper right). That on the south is ca. 0.12 m. high, while on the northwest it varies from 0.05 to 0.12 m. The wall between 2 and 7 is only one course high, but it rests on a ledge that is 0.18 m. high on the side of Room 2. The rock floor of the room is 0.14 m. lower than it had been in I.4, and this gives a clear ledge cutting for the wall between 2 and 8. We have already noted the doorway connecting Rooms 1 and 2; there was also a doorway

between 2 and 3, and there was most probably one between 2 and 8 as well, but of this nothing remains. The rock floor is at − 6.94 m. and on it was the burned debris of the house, including fragments of several amphoroid kraters and two jugs of plain ware, a jug with pointed base (B875), a whorl (B1612), a pierced stone disc (B1548), a mace-head, a quern and a grinder.

The rock was also cut down in the area of Room 3, leaving a ledge 0.14 m. high for the wall between it and Room 2 (pl. 13a, upper left). A bit of the northeast wall is preserved, and it is assumed that there was a doorway between 3 and 4. Nothing is known of the south and northwest walls; for the former we have continued the line of the wall between 1 and 2, for the latter the line of the cliff wall. The rock floor, at − 7.16 m., was covered with the usual burned debris; a bucchero jug (B693) lay on the threshold within the doorway to Room 2.

Room 4 covers much the same area as Room I.6, though the trench for wall 4-7 is farther southeast than that for I.6-3. There was still some 0.04 m. of LC II debris above the rock floor of I.6, which was cut into for the wall between Rooms 4 and 7. The wall between 4 and 5 is also a little farther to the northeast than the wall I.6-7, so that the floor at − 6.74 m. goes a bit over the old wall for I.6-7. There are no indications for the northeast and northwest walls of Room 4. Burned debris filled the room above the − 6.74 m. floor.

Of Room 5, little remains but the rock cutting, 0.12 m. deep, for the wall between 5 and 6, which seems to continue the line of the wall between Rooms 2 and 3. There was LC IIIA debris down to the floor at − 6.62 m., while burned debris was found above the − 6.54 m. level in Room 5. Room 6 is hypothetical as well, except for its wall with Room 5. The burned debris above − 6.54 m. occurs here as well. Only the northwestern part of Room 7 is preserved, with a clear cutting for the wall with Room 4 and preserved masonry for the wall with Room 2. There is no evidence for the room beyond the wall between Rooms 2 and 8. There was a *chavara* floor at − 6.83 m., above which was burned debris. Like Room I.3, Room VII.7 may have been a courtyard, though it was somewhat narrower than the former.

For Room 8 there is only the southwest wall

built over the cobble pavement of Room I.4, making 8 a long, narrow room, though how long is uncertain. A white plaster floor at − 6.47 m. went to the preserved wall; it was just under topsoil. Room 9 may not have been a room at all; possibly it was a court. Other than the preserved masonry walls, there was part of a plaster floor in the eastern part of the area at − 6.92 m.

It would seem that House VII retained the tripartite division of House I, but with narrower central and southwestern parts. It seems also that House VII retained the rectangularity of House I as well, except in the western part where it adapted itself to the 30-degree change in the orientation of House V, to which it was attached in part, and the area of which it may have used after House V was gone. The destruction of House VII was undoubtedly by fire, still within the LC IIIA period. In the area of Room 9, as well as that of Room V.4, a series of Geometric-Archaic cuttings were exposed (Benson 1970, 32, No. 11), rare evidence for occupation later than LC IIIA in Area E.

THE HEARTH AREA
Benson 1970, 32-35

To the south of the south corner of House IV, and as far as the rock outcrop at the very south corner of Area E, there was a deep and large depression, at least part of which was man-made by cutting back the rock. Here Daniel found a whole series of hearths, often one above the other and scattered through an area of about 20 square meters (fig. 21) and at levels from − 10.15 to − 9.72 m. Benson has published Daniel's detailed description of the hearth at − 9.87 m., a drawing of which is given in figure 22. Though Benson enlarged this area, he found that the hearths did not extend beyond Daniel's dig. In his description of the material from this area, Benson (1970, 34) mentions a metal mold, or molds (B1595-1600), and numerous fragments of crucibles (B1550-1557), indicating that the hearths were parts of smelting furnaces from a small, local copper smelting industry, which existed here during the LC IIB and IIC phases. The area was filled in during LC IIC and the trenches for the walls of the southeastern part of House VIII were cut into this fill during LC IIIA.

HOUSE E.VIII (pls. 13c-d; 14a-c)
Benson 1969, 27-28; D:1g, D:2e and D:2f

House VIII does not fit into either main category of house plans known at Bamboula, the L-shaped plan or the rectangular plan with tripartite divisions. The house extends into the undug area southwest of Area E, and knowing its entire plan might possibly help to explain some of the anomalies. While most of the northwest-southeast walls are parallel to those of House IV, with which House VIII shares a party wall, and the cross walls are largely at right angles to these, there are departures, most notably in the northwest wall of the house. This may be due to the fact that the rock face here goes to the west, while the house wall may have taken the direction of the 79 m. contour line at this point. It is in the southeastern part of the house that there is a slight general shift in the direction of the walls of about 5 degrees counterclockwise. Much of this area is over the fill in the rock depression, while all the rest of the house is founded on rock. Another unusual feature in House VIII is the number of small rooms, for which we have no explanation. A considerable quantity of masonry is preserved in this house, partly because some walls are founded in trenches in the fill over the Hearth Area and also because in general the level of the rock is lower and the depth of the fill is deeper than in House IV. These walls, together with rock cuttings for others, make the perimeters of most rooms sure. The outer wall, on the northwest, is preserved for only one course, but is composed of many large stones, some laid as headers through the wall. Similar construction is to be observed in the section of wall preserved between Rooms 1 and 5; there is also a large stone laid as a header in the wall 2-3.

The very large area in the northern corner of the house, called Room 1, was most likely a courtyard; there is no indication of any subdivision of this area, which is over 6.00 m. wide (pl. 13c). A drain-like cutting in the north corner, parallel to the party wall and very close to it, which went through the northwest wall, would confirm this identification. The line of the northwest wall has been taken as the continuation of that of the preserved stretch of masonry and this brings the wall exactly to the corner of House IV as marked by the rock cutting. The northeast wall was the southwest wall of House IV, which is preserved to within a meter of the corner; the possibility of a post here has already been mentioned (p. 44). A cutting in the rock suggests that another post, or buttress, was placed against this wall in the east angle of Room 1, at the entrance to Room 2. There was no wall between 1 and 2, though there was probably a rock cutting in the line of the northwest side of the wall 1-3. The line of the wall 1-5 is marked by an irregular cutting on the side of 1, by the small stretch of masonry and by a row of three post holes on the side of 5. The room has a *chavara* floor at −9.22 m. Accumulation on this floor was of the LC IIIA phase (Benson 1969 D:1g) up to −9.20 m., while above this was the building debris, including some burnt debris.

The small Room 2 is delimited by the party wall on the northeast, the thick wall with 3 on the southwest, a rock cutting on the northwest and the edge of its pavement on the southeast. A large, oval hole that goes slightly under the party wall at about the center of the room was the entrance to a large cave which extended under IV.4 and was apparently used as a cellar. Building debris was found down to the −8.67 m. level but no lower levels are given.

Room 3 is another small room with a shape similar to that of Room 2, but it is even smaller. It has its full northwest wall and a bit of its northeast wall preserved because they were founded in trenches on fill, while the southeastern two-thirds of the room is on rock, and the earth here was very shallow (pl. 13d). There is rock cutting for the rest of the northeast wall, and the edge of a plaster floor gives the line of the southeast wall. Only a small corner of masonry, just at the southeast side of the doorway into Room 4, gives the line of the southwest wall. There are fine, drafted threshold blocks for this wide doorway, 1.20 m., which is also framed by well-squared blocks in the west outer corner of the room and in the northwest wall (pl. 14a). The lowest floor was of *chavara*, on which was early accumulation from the use of the house, then a floor at −8.96 m. with building debris above it.

Room 4 seems to have been nothing more than a narrow passage leading to a cellar entrance at its southeast end. The edge of the excavated area is just to the southwest of the cellar-cave entrance,

and one can only conjecture that the wall between 4 and 5 continued here to meet the wall between 4 and 7, which is preserved just to the edge of the area. There seems to have been a *chavara* floor and then a broad staircase cut into the rock that led into the cave; this was filled in before House VIII was built, in LC II, with almost no intrusive LC III pottery to indicate any use of the cellar contemporary with House VIII.

Only a narrow strip along the northeast side of Room 5 has been excavated and only its northwest and northeast wall lines are known, the latter with the three post holes on the side of Room 5.

Room 6 is of an irregular shape, though all of its wall lines are known except that with Room 7. As we have noted, the western part of the room is over rock, the eastern part over fill in a deep depression. The party wall is preserved for most of the length of Room 6 and the southeast wall for its entire length. Off the latter, only a few stones may mark the direction of the wall 6-7. The walls with Rooms 2, 3 and 4 are known, as already indicated. There was a packed earth floor at −8.78 m., over which was a very shallow accumulation from the period of use of the room and then the usual building debris. With no doors preserved to any of the six adjoining rooms, the use of Room 6 eludes us, but it was the largest room in House VIII after the courtyard.

There is little to say of Room 7, only partially excavated. Its northwest wall is largely preserved, almost to the edge of the excavation, and there is a bit of its northeast wall. The line of the southeast wall is given by a rock cutting, which shows it to be a continuation of the southeast wall of Room 6. A 1954 extension of the trench to the southwest revealed a section of masonry for this wall.

The series of three small rooms, 8-10, that form the southeast side of House VIII, are all built over the deep deposit in which the series of hearths were found. The walls for all these rooms were founded in deep trenches through this accumulated deposit, so that their line is certain even where the masonry is not preserved, as in the northeast and southeast walls of Room 8. It was originally thought that these rooms may have been an addition to House VIII, but the manner in which Rooms 8 and 9 repeat the pattern of Rooms 2 and 3 would suggest that they were contemporary. The slight change in the direction of their walls, some 5 degrees, has already been mentioned.

The northwest and southwest walls of Room 8 are preserved for some 0.65 to 0.70 m. above the floor at −9.46 m., which is about 0.70 m. below the floor of Room 6 (pl. 14b). On this floor is a bin of clay and stones, lined with *chavara* plaster; it sits against the wall with Room 9 and close to the narrow doorway that connects the two rooms. On the floor there was again the usual 0.02 m. of accumulation from the period of use and then the building debris up to −9.13 m.; above this, to −8.95 m., was a post-destruction deposit which was still of LC III date. Below the floor was the deep LC II accumulation in which were the hearths.

Room 9 has all its walls, though there was disturbance at the east corner; most of the walls are preserved for a height of ca. 0.30 m. above the floor at −9.44 m., which was of *chavara* plaster. This floor was ca. 0.70-0.80 m. below the rock floor of Room 6. Over this floor was the same accumulation as in Room 8.

A large outcropping of rock occupied the south end of Room 10 (pl. 14c). The southwest side of the room remains unexcavated, so that the cleared area is very small. The wall with 9 is fully preserved and there is a spur wall from it to the rock outcropping. The line of the wall with 7 is determined by a cutting in the rock on the side of 7. Since the corner formed by these two walls, the east corner of Room 10, lies over the south corner of Room 9, it is likely that these walls of 10 mark a second construction phase for House VIII. There was possibly a door at the northwest end of the wall 9-10, with a step down to 9, for the floor of 10, paved with large flagstones, still preserved in the southeast half of the room, was at −9.22 m. (pl. 14c). The rock mass in the southern corner of the room has three rock-cut stairs in it, which probably led out to the street from the flagstone-paved court that was Room 10. This may have formed the entrance to House VIII, from Room 10 into 9 and then up into 6, though there is no sign of the step that would have been needed here. Another possibility is an entryway from 10 to 7 and then 6, which would require less of a step between the two levels.

While the three rooms in the southeastern part of the house seem to have been part of the original construction, the low level of at least two of them, 8 and 9, might suggest that these were basement rooms, entered from 10, and there could have been a room, or rooms, over them with an entrance from 6. The combination of Rooms 2 and 3, less than 2.00 m. wide, has also suggested to me the possibility that there was a stairway here leading to an upper storey, which would have been above 6, 8 and 9, at least. Area 6 then, paved with packed earth, may have been a stable, entered from the courtyard 1 through 4. For all of this there is no evidence other than the logic of the plan and elevations. Without exposing the rest of the house, much about House VIII must remain conjecture.

CHAPTER V

CONCLUSIONS: BAMBOULA AND LATE CYPRIOTE ARCHITECTURE

HOUSE FORMS AT BAMBOULA

Bamboula began to be settled early in the Late Cypriote period; before that the area was apparently used only sparingly as a cemetery going back to Early Cypriote times. In the two large areas excavated on the lower slopes of Bamboula, Areas A and E, building operations began in the LC IA phase, early in the sixteenth century B.C. In both areas, occupation was continuous through LC IIIA, to the beginning of the twelfth century B.C., or some four hundred years. Only in Area A did occupation continue during the next period, LC IIIB, a half century during which A.V and A.VI were rebuilt and A.VIII was the only new construction. The one house in Area D, to the southwest of Area E and at about the same level, was not constructed until the LC IIIA period. The fragmentary remains of dwellings in Trench 15, Area B, belong at the earliest to LC IIB, the late fourteenth and early thirteenth century B.C. The great well higher up the slope may have been constructed in the previous LC IIA phase. If any pattern is detectable, it is that the settlement remained along the lower contours of Bamboula, below the 83 m. contour, for the first two centuries of its existence, and began to occupy the higher slopes only after 1400 B.C.

Area E offers the best sequence of houses, eight in all. There were eventually the same number of houses in Area A, but very little is preserved of the three earliest buildings, and A.IV, built in the LC IIB phase, has not been exposed to a sufficient extent to enable us to know the type of its plan. We know, therefore, the house types in Area A only from LC IIC on, when A.V was built, and it offers us the earliest example of the L-shaped plan; all the earlier houses, in Area E, were of the rectangular type with tripartite division. The following table gives the division of the houses according to the two main types of plan.

Rectangular-Tripartite		L-Shaped		Unknown
E.I	LC 1A	A.V	LC IIC	A.IV
E.II	LC 1A	A.VII	LC IIIA	E.VIII
E.III	LC IIB	D.I	LC IIIA	
E.IV	LC IIC	A.VIII	LC IIIB	
E.V	LC IIC			
E.VI	LC IIC (squeezed)			
E.VII	LC IIIA			
A.VI	LC IIIA			

Clearly, the dominant type of house plan during four centuries of settlement on Bamboula was the rectangular house with three main divisions running through the depth of the house, each of these then subdivided into two rooms in most cases, but into three or four rooms in other instances. In most examples, the central division of the three is wider than the side divisions; only in House E.IV are all three divisions of the same width, and in no case are the side divisions wider than the central one. As for the subdivision of these three parts, there are two main patterns. Both Houses E.I and A.VI show a division into long room and short room, occupying about two-thirds and one-third of the depth of the house respectively, and these two houses represent the earliest and latest in the series. In both of these houses, there is good evidence that there was a second storey over the small rooms, very likely with a balcony in front of them which gave access to the three rooms of the upper storey; at the same time, the balcony roofed the back part of the large central room, which in almost all instances seems to have been a courtyard. Both Houses E.V and E.VII seem to have had a similar uneven division in depth of the three divisions in width, but in neither case is there evidence for a second storey. In House E.IV, the two parts are close to equal, while in Houses E.II and E.III they are equal. Again, there is no compelling reason to believe that any of these houses with equal, or almost equal, divisions in depth had a second storey.

The second type of house plan, which is L-shaped, is known in only four examples at Bamboula, and of these two may be doubtful. We know this type of plan also from Bamboula only in LC IIC, LC IIIA and LC IIIB. The most typical example of the L-shaped plan is to be seen in House A.V (fig. 5). Like an L, houses of this type have two unequal arms, which meet in a common, corner room. They usually have two more rooms in one arm and one in the other; the corner room is contracted in its extension along the short arm so as to permit access from the other room in the short arm to the next room in the long arm. The area within the angle of the L typically has a room built in it that does not extend the full length of the long arm of the L. If House D.I is indeed an L-shaped house, it is a variant which

has two small rooms both in the short arm of the L and in the angle. House A.VIII, on the other hand, seems to have had no room in the angle. From the examples at Bamboula, then, there is far less consistency among the houses with L-shaped plan than among those with the rectangular plan with tripartite division. While the rectangular houses seem always to have contained a courtyard, around three sides of which the house was built, the L-shaped houses had an exterior courtyard; the concept of the two types of plan is thus totally different. The L-shaped houses are much more compact and usually are smaller than those with rectangular plan. Even here, however, there is wide variation, for House A.VI is a quite small rectangular house and House D.I may have been as large as the rectangular houses in Area E. The difference in size may thus be a function of neighborhood rather than house type, for the houses in Area E were in all periods larger on the average than those in Area A.

There are distinct differences in planning of house complexes between Areas A and E. As we have seen, the series of rectangular houses in Area E proceeded in blocks delimited by streets, the location of which was determined at least in part by the tombs underlying the streets. The series E.I, II and III represents three houses in a block delimited by streets on the northeast, southeast and southwest and the cliff on the northwest. The beginning of another similar block is to be seen with the construction of E.IV. There followed the destruction of II and III and the re-use of the area they had occupied by one large house, E.V, still of the same rectangular type, but with a different orientation. The addition of E.VI in the resultant angle introduced the first relatively small house in an area which had always known quite large residences. The remodeling of E.I, with an extension running into a second unoccupied triangular area over E.II, resulted in an even larger house, still essentially of the rectangular type. In all of this rebuilding, the integrity of the original block was retained, with only a slight infringement onto the Street of the Tombs by House E.VI. This area remained from beginning to end occupied by large houses, almost entirely of the rectangular type.

The history of the residential development in Area A is different in many respects. We know very little of the first three houses, which were built farther to the northeast than the later ones. They seem to have been destroyed in the clearing of the area prior to the construction of the Circuit Wall and the street back of it in LC IIB. Only then did the new block of houses begin to develop with the building of Houses A.IV, V and VI, (fig. 23), one next to the other from northwest to southeast, using party walls, as is the case with the first three houses built in Area E. Those in Area A are much smaller houses. A.IV may have been of the L-shaped type; it certainly was not rectangular. A.V was L-shaped and is our best example of the type at Bamboula, but it too is a small house, certainly not more than 50 square meters, excluding the court, which was on the back of the house away from the street entrance. House A.VI, built next, is our smallest example of the rectangular type. There is a similarity in the series A.IV, V and VI and E.I, II and III in the building of houses in series with party walls between them.

We know only the street in front of the block in Area A, for the unexcavated area cuts off both sides of this block. There apparently was no street on the southwest side of these houses, for the courtyard of A.V is in back of the house, and soon A.VIa was built at the back of A.VI, to be replaced later by A.VIII. Thus, the similarity between Areas A and E ends with the sequence of three houses built in a row. It is not impossible that the courtyards of the L-shaped houses faced onto a street, parallel to the one along the Circuit Wall, but beyond the area of excavations; this must remain speculative. Though Areas A and E were occupied through the same time span, were part of the same settlement, and were only a little more than 100 m. apart, still, the dissimilarities with respect to town planning between the two areas seem greater than the similarities. Area E gives a definite impression of more spaciousness, of more controlled planning and, by inference, of greater wealth.

CONSTRUCTION METHODS AND MATERIALS

There are differences, too, in the construction of the houses in the two areas. In the earlier houses of Area E, the walls are 0.70 to 0.80 m. thick and the party wall of I-II runs to 1.20 m. By the time Houses III and IV were built, some of the interior walls between small rooms were only 0.60 m. thick, but outer walls, especially party walls, remained more substantial. In the smaller House E.VI, wedged into a triangular area in the LC IIC period, the walls are only 0.60 m. thick. Wall thickness seems thus to have been a function of size, as one would expect, but construction was less substantial in the later periods than in the early ones. A thickness of 0.60 m. is the average for almost all the walls of the houses in Area A; some are even as thin as 0.50 m. True, all the houses are smaller, but even where a second storey is suspected, as in A.VI, the walls are not thicker. We did notice several instances in Area A in which walls had to be strengthened during rebuildings or remodelings, an indication of weaknesses in the original construction.

Because of the very different nature of the base on which the house foundations were laid in Areas A and E, the preservation varies greatly. The houses of Area A have their foundations on bedrock in most instances, but foundation trenches were cut for them through fill in many cases and the foundations then laid in them. In such construction, either the foundations or the trenches are likely to survive. In Area E, the houses were built almost entirely on rock, except for those small areas where there were depressions in the rock, which had to be filled, and then the walls were founded as in Area A. Otherwise, the rock was cut down, usually leaving a ledge or shelf on which the wall foundations were laid. Though most of the walls are gone, for the depth of fill over the rock in most of Area E was negligible, the rock ledges attest their line and thickness. In the case of party walls in Area E, and particularly where there was a difference in general level of the houses, as between I and II and II and III, the walls were usually founded on a shelf at the higher level. Sometimes in the rebuilding of party walls, the wall foundation began with the lower level of the new house. In instances where one house was built over another, as with E.VI over E.III, the foundation trenches were sunk through the fill over the floors of the earlier house and founded on the earlier floors.

It is clear that earlier masonry, in evidence

largely in Area E, was more carefully built than was later masonry. Stones were larger and were more carefully chosen for their quasi-rectangular shape; more attention was given to coursing. In a few instances there was use of white clay binder, but mostly the foundations were laid dry and, when the stones were square, without the use of small stones in the interstices. One very large stone, 0.80 by 1.00 m. (which was retrieved from a pit into which it had been thrown, thereby preserving it from being broken up for re-use), is dressed much in the manner of Greek Cyclopean masonry; it has been placed on the foundation for the party wall between E.I and II, from which it may originally have derived (pl. 14d). With time, and with the building of smaller houses, as in Area A, less care was taken with the masonry of foundations—stones were smaller and largely unhewn, little attention was given to coursing and, because of the irregularity of the stones, more chips and rubble were used for chinking. In some instances where the top row of stones of the foundations extended above the house floors and was thus meant to be seen, greater care was taken in the choice of blocks, and they were more closely fitted. Care was usually taken at the corners and at the sides of doorways to use squared blocks of greater size, often running through the thickness of the wall. Bonding of one foundation with another was rare; it was more usual to have walls abutting than bonding.

There was much re-use of material from earlier foundations. When one building was to be superimposed on another, it was usual for the builders to leave parts of old foundations that could be incorporated into new ones and to rip out the other stones from their foundation trenches so as to use them again. Apparently even bricks were re-used when they remained whole. There are a number of instances of re-used floors and, in general, one gets the impression of economy in the use of materials that demanded the re-use of any and all available materials.

On the stone foundations were built walls of sun-dried mud brick, which seem to have comprised the standard type of wall in all periods. The standard brick was about 0.60 by 0.40 by 0.12 m., though from the platform in A.VI.3 come bricks that are 0.63 by 0.33 by 0.12 m. There is an instance in A.IV in which the mud-

brick wall was laid on a flat bedding of beaten earth; this, to be sure, was an interior wall. There are a number of cases in which such mud-brick walls were strengthened by wooden posts set in post holes along the edge of the foundation. There is even one case, in the west corner of E.IV, in which a large wooden post may have been set in the angle of two mud-brick walls for added support. Another method of adding support was to build a small spur wall, or buttress, against the wall; these seem to have been more in the nature of repairs or part of remodeling.

Brick walls were sometimes coated with clay or lime plaster; one of the most careful examples of the latter is in A.VIII.3, where all the walls are so coated and the coating is continuous with the lime floor. There is an excellent, but unique, example in House D.I.4 of the use of orthostates to protect the lower part of a brick wall (pl. 9b), the upper part of which seems then to have been covered with plaster.

There is much variety in the material used for floors of rooms. The leveled rock was sometimes used and often this required the filling of irregularities, which were then surfaced with clay or plaster. Floors of brown earth, dark red clay or packed sandy clay are known; in later phases the leveled accumulation over earlier floors was made to serve as a floor. A layer of plaster over the bedrock was a common means of making it smoother. Floors of *chavara*, crushed sandstone, were very common and this material was sometimes mixed with plaster; lime plaster was used by itself in many instances for floors. More unusual types of flooring are flagstones, as in A.VI.5, pebbles or cobbles, seen in E.I.4, stone chips and potsherds, used in E.III.1, and large, flat sea pebbles and sherds covering different parts of E.V.4.

In addition to the walls, the ceilings or roofs of the houses were sometimes supported by posts, single or multiple, which rested on stones set into or on the floors. A cylindrical stone in A.IV.3 had a depression cut into the top surface which would take a post 0.155 by 0.165 m. Flat stones were embedded in many of the floors for this purpose. In one instance, two large flat stones were set one above the other as a pillar base. Down the center of E.II.2 was a row of post holes with flat stones between them. It is possible that posts set in holes were also used for roof supports, but in this instance it may have been the flat stones that served such a purpose, while the holes held posts that were part of a light structure built within the court.

Doorways varied greatly in width, from as little as 0.50 m. to as much as 1.55 m. Often there was no door, as in the widest doorways, and such doorways may have had no threshold; rather, the floor ran through the doorway. In many cases, however, the presence of a door is shown by the pivot stone found on one side of the doorway. We have no case of two pivot stones, one on either side of the doorway, indicating the use of double doors, but this does not preclude their use. The door jambs were often carefully fitted with slabs of stone the width of the wall and rather thin, usually unhewn but specially selected. In the doorway A.V.3-4 the jamb was a rectangular block of limestone, unhewn but quite regular, which was found standing on end. A large block of calcareous sandstone, 0.60 by 0.22 by 0.15 m., used at the side of a doorway in A.VIII.1, shows evidence of having been cut with a saw. There is evidence for the use of a wooden jamb in the doorway A.V.3-5. For the thresholds, it was common to use a row of large stones, selected to give an even surface. In the doorway A.V.3-4 a row of river stones was used. One of the finest thresholds was in the doorway E.VIII.3-4, where two large squared blocks were used. There was evidence for a wooden threshold in the doorway A.IV.1-3, which was 0.15 m. wide and 0.08 m. deep. The position of doorways was usually in, or very close to, the corner of a room; there are rarer examples of doorways in the center of a room. The main entrance to a house was often a wide doorway, probably with double doors, leading from the street to the court in the rectangular houses. Doorways were frequently blocked up with masonry when buildings were remodeled, though it was common to re-use them and to raise the threshold.

We have conjectured the presence of a second storey in at least two of the houses—E.I and A.VI. In the latter, in Room 5, there were found two blocks of stone which may well have formed the bottom steps of a stairway leading to the second floor; presumably the rest of the staircase was built of wood, as was the balcony to which it led. There is the possibility that staircases existed in E.III.1 and E.IV.4 as well, and a second storey has been conjectured over part of E.VIII.

The roofs of these houses probably had a slight slope and were built with wooden rafters; over this was laid straw or matting, which then bore a thick layer of soft white clay, called *konnos*. A lot of fallen debris in House A.VI gives evidence of such a roof, with the clay at least 0.10 m. thick. When well packed, this material gives an impervious roof that is easy to keep in repair. Such roofs are still common today on houses in Cyprus (pl. 14e), just one example of the very long and continued use of some building methods on the island.

Many of the rooms of these houses were fitted with a variety of appurtenances, often indicating the particular use to which a room was put. Some of the larger of these were long benches or platforms built against a wall, or in a corner, sometimes in stone but often of brick coated with clay. The stone covers of some were sometimes removable and the space beneath was used for storage. There were smaller bins of brick and/or stone, as in A.VIII.1, or double bins, as in A.VIII.5. Both A.VI.5 and A.VII.1 had ovens, while in A.VI.6 and A.VII.12 there were fireplaces. Instead of small structures built on the floors, pits of various kinds were often dug into the floor. Bothroi, sometimes quite large, were used as refuse pits; smaller pits often held storage jars or other vases; there were pits which may have been used for storage and which at times were covered with stone slabs. The deepest digging was for wells, found in A.VI.5 and E.II.6. The former, 3.10 m. deep, had an oval shape and footholds cut into opposite sides; the latter was 5.00 m. deep. The great square well at the top of Bamboula, 18.05 m. deep, had its bottom at −20.96 m., giving a definite idea of the depth of the water table. The smaller wells in the houses apparently found water-bearing levels higher up that were sufficient for a single house, whereas the great well was most likely a community development. There was only one instance of a drain cut into one of the house floors, in A.VII.10; it was lined and covered with stone slabs. There is also a drain through the wall in the north corner of E.VIII.

Many of the houses had cellars, which were natural depressions in the rock, used either as they were or cut to give more usable space. That in Area D is the best example, but there are others under E.VIII. An even larger cavelike opening under E.IV.1 and 2 may possibly have served as a stable. All of these underground chambers are in Areas D and E, where the nature of the rock made large depressions available for use.

The picture of the domestic economy was made fairly complete by the many objects found on the floors of the houses, some of them fallen from a second storey. Pottery was much the most numer-ous category and there was a great variety of storage vessels, some used for cooking and others for eating and drinking. Querns and rubbing stones were found frequently; there were also whetstones. Loomweights often designate the room used for weaving. It is a picture not very different from that of the rural economy of villages in Cyprus today.

COMPARATIVE MATERIAL

THE RECTANGULAR-TRIPARTITE HOUSE IN CYPRUS

The earlier of the two main house types at Bamboula, that with rectangular-tripartite plan, is known elsewhere on Cyprus; at no other site, how-ever, does it appear as early as at Bamboula, where it occurs already in LC IA, shortly after 1600 B.C. The earliest house of this type outside of Bamboula I take to be House B at Morphou–Toumba tou Skourou, apparently built first at the beginning of the fifteenth century B.C. and with its final phase at the end of the thirteenth cen-tury B.C.[1] Though the south side of this house is largely destroyed, it appears to have the main features of the rectangular-tripartite house. It has not yet been interpreted as such by the excavators and can only be included here subject to further study by them. It is a large house, about 110 square meters within the outer walls, comparable to the houses in Area E at Bamboula.

The three other houses of the rectangular-tri-partite type which I know from Cyprus were all built first in the LC IIIA period, just after 1200 B.C., and so are contemporary with the two latest houses of this type from Bamboula, A.VI and E.VII. The one at Pyla-Kokkinokremos, Area II,[2] excavated by Dikaios in 1952 and 1954, is as carefully rectangular as the early Bamboula ex-amples; like them it has six rooms, but the middle room at the back is not as wide as the central court in front, and the plan thus lacks the strict tripartite division so characteristic of the Bam-boula houses. The house at Pyla-Kokkinokremos seems to have had a court in front of it in addition to the court within the house, into which led the main entrance from the outer court. The area of the house, taken inside the outer walls, is about 90 square meters, median between the extremes noted at Bamboula. Another house, possibly of similar type, adjoins this house on the southeast and the two share a party wall; on the northwest there was apparently a court of still another house. Dikaios has suggested the possibility of a second storey over part of this house, with a wooden staircase leading up to it. With slight variations, then, this house is very close in plan to the rec-tangular-tripartite houses from Bamboula.

At Enkomi, it is a unit of the Ashlar Building in Area I, comprising Rooms 2, 3, 6, 6A, 7 and 8, which conforms most closely to the rectangular-tripartite house type.[3] On the ground floor, at least, this unit had no communication with the rest of the large, quasi-rectangular complex; Dikaios, however, suggested that there may have been some connection at the second-floor level, which he postulated over some of the rooms of this unit. Here the three back rooms are just half as long as the front rooms, a pattern seen most clearly in Houses E.I and A.VI at Bamboula. On the anal-ogy of the Bamboula houses, it could be expected that a second storey would have existed over Rooms 6A, 7 and 8 of the Enkomi house. The wall between Rooms 7 and 8 is not in line with that between Rooms 2 and 3, breaking the uni-formity of the tripartite division; this is exactly the same variation that was seen at Pyla-Kokkinokremos. The unit has an area of ca. 65 square meters, very close to that of the smallest house of this type at Bamboula, A.VI.

1. Vermeule 1974, 9-10, Fig. 4. For the dates, see Chronique des Fouilles, "Morphou–Toumba tou Skou-rou," *Bulletin de correspondance hellénique* 98 (1974) 862.

2. Dikaios 1971, 900-907, Pls. 295.6 and 296.6.

3. Dikaios 1969, 172-73, 181-82, Pls. 273-75.

The recently excavated house in Area 8 at Hala Sultan Tekke[4] seems again to be of the rectangular-tripartite type, though the northeast corner of the building is not preserved, and so one cannot be sure of the exact plan. Room 4, however, at the center of the west side is a court, flanked by Rooms 1 and 2 and with the main entrance to the house on its west side. Room 3, behind Room 2, is shorter in depth than the latter, and this seems to have been the rule for the other rooms on the east side of the house. This would indicate the possibility of a second storey over the back rooms, but no evidence for a staircase leading to it has yet been mentioned by the excavators. This is a large house, with an area inside the exterior walls of ca. 130 square meters, comparable to some of the larger houses of Area E at Bamboula. There is apparently another house to the south of this one, sharing a party wall with it.

Thus we have four houses in Cyprus, outside of Bamboula, which are sufficiently close in plan to the rectangular-tripartite houses of Bamboula to be classed with them. Geographically, this house type was widespread in the island, from Toumba tou Skourou on the west to Enkomi in the east, and from these sites on the north to Pyla-Kokkinokremos and Hala Sultan Tekke, in the Larnaca district, and Bamboula on the south. In time, rectangular-tripartite house types occurred through almost the entire Late Cypriote period, though perhaps not in its very last phase. It can be considered one of the most typical house plans of Cyprus in the Late Bronze Age, possibly the most typical.

Thus far, there are no antecedents for the rectangular-tripartite house plan in Cyprus before its first appearance in the LC IA period at Bamboula. Lacking, also, are any houses of similar plan from Bronze Age Greece, Anatolia or the Near East. At present, this house type appears to be unique to Cyprus of the Late Bronze Age. Yet, in many respects, it has a plan that is remarkably similar to the pastas-type house of Classical and Hellenistic Greece, best known from Olynthus.[5] Åström has already pointed this out with respect to the house at Pyla-Kokkinokremos,[6]

where the comparison is particularly apt because of the corridor running the full width of the house in front of the three rear rooms. Like the pastas-type house, houses of Bronze Age Cyprus often had a second storey over the three rear rooms, though there is no evidence for a second storey over the rooms flanking the court, which was usual in the pastas-type house. Robinson knows of no antecedents for the pastas-type house earlier than its first appearance at Olynthus in the fifth century B.C.[7] There is thus a gap of some seven centuries between the latest rectangular-tripartite houses of Late Bronze Age Cyprus and the earliest pastas-type houses of Olynthus, and there is at present no way of connecting the two similar types. Nonetheless, one is struck by the similarity and can only point it out.

THE L-SHAPED HOUSE IN CYPRUS

The L-shaped house type of Bamboula occurs there first in House A.V of the LC IIIA period, the late thirteenth and early twelfth centuries B.C. It is this house which offers the archetypal L-shaped plan: the long arm has three or more rooms, the short arm two rooms, counting the corner room twice; the corner room is as wide as one arm but less wide than the other, allowing direct communication between the two rooms adjacent to it without going through the corner room; the angle is filled by a room that has one of its sides roughly in line with the end of the short arm of the L, but the other side falls short of the long arm; the house has an exterior court. Strictly speaking, only House A.V conforms completely to this type, but House D.I., also dated to LC IIIA, seems to be an enlargement and elaboration of the type, with more rooms in the arms and the angle. We may possibly see the elements of an L-shaped house in the large complex that is called House A.VII (Rooms 4 to 10). House A.VIII is L-shaped, but seems to have had no room in the angle; it is the latest house built at Bamboula and belongs to the LC IIIB period. Thus, there are fewer examples of the L-shaped house than of the rectangular-tripartite type, as well as less uniformity in plan among them.

While House A at Apliki–Karamallos in north-

---

4. Hult 1978, 30-31, Figs. 39-45.
5. Robinson 1940.
6. Åström 1972, 20.

7. Robinson 1940, col. 266.

west Cyprus has an L-shaped plan,[8] built along two sides of its court, it does not relate in its essential characteristics to the type at Bamboula—the scheme of arrangement of the rooms in the two arms of the L is different and there is no corner room. The whole concept is thus quite different, and the Apliki house cannot be said to offer a parallel to those at Bamboula. Since the house was constructed first in LC IIC, about a century earlier than the earliest L-shaped houses at Bamboula, it may represent an earlier type, from which the Bamboula type developed.

A house of EC IIIB found at Alambra in central Cyprus[9] has been mentioned as having the same L-shaped plan as those at Bamboula and Apliki.[10] In fact, it consists of two roughly rectangular rooms, adjoining but not communicating, one larger than the other and thus forming an L-shaped plan. There would seem to be no possible similarity between this house plan and the concept of the L-shaped plan epitomized by House A.V at Bamboula, or even such a plan as that of House A at Apliki.

In fact, no other site in Cyprus offers a good parallel for the type of L-shaped plan seen in a few houses at Bamboula. This would seem, again,

to be a local development, possibly related to an earlier tendency to an L-shaped plan noted in House A at Apliki. Nor have I found any houses of the Late Bronze Age, or earlier, from East Mediterranean areas that might be related in concept to the house type epitomized by A.V at Bamboula.

The fourteen Late Cypriote houses listed in the table at the beginning of these conclusions form the largest group of this period thus far reported, excluding the much larger and more monumental structures at Enkomi, which may not have been solely for domestic usage. The Bamboula houses cover almost the entire range of the Late Cypriote period, except for its latest phase. The rectangular-tripartite house clearly appears to have been the main type in use throughout this period, both here and elsewhere in Cyprus. The L-shaped house, on the contrary, appears first only in LC IIC, and has a much more limited use at Bamboula, as well as in the rest of the island. A couple of houses may not conform to either type, though their plans are incomplete. The Bamboula houses give an excellent idea of what must have been the average dwelling of Late Cypriote times, of some of the more permanent accoutrements of such houses, and of much of the movable equipment used in them in everyday life. The picture is one of a not uncomfortable life style which seems to have taken full advantage of available materials, as well as of a benign climate.

8. Taylor 1952, 133-44.
9. Gjerstad 1926, 19-27, Fig. 1.
10. Åström 1972, 29.

BIBLIOGRAPHY

Åström, Paul
1972
Swedish Cyprus Expedition, Vol. IV, part IC. *The Late Cypriote Bronze Age Architecture and Pottery.* Lund.

Benson, J. L.
1969
"Bamboula at Kourion, The Stratification of the Settlement." *Report of the Department of Antiquities, Cyprus:* 1-28.

1970
"Bamboula at Kourion, The Stratification of the Settlement." *Report of the Department of Antiquities, Cyprus:* 25-74.

1972
Bamboula at Kourion. The Necropolis and the Finds. Philadelphia.

1973
The Necropolis of Kaloriziki. Göteborg.

Daniel, John Franklin
1937
"Kourion—The Late Bronze Age Settlement." *University of Pennsylvania Museum Bulletin* 7 (1): 15-18.

1938
"Excavations at Kourion. The Late Bronze Age Settlement—Provisional Report." *American Journal of Archaeology* 42: 261-75.

1939a
"The Inscribed Pithoi from Kourion." *American Journal of Archaeology* 43: 102-3.

1939b
"Kourion: The Late Bronze Age Settlement." *University of Pennsylvania Museum Bulletin* 7 (3): 14-21.

1940
"The Achaeans at Kourion." *University of Pennsylvania Museum Bulletin* 8 (1): 3-14.

1941
"Prolegomena to the Cypro-Minoan Script." *American Journal of Archaeology* 45: 249-82.

1943
Reviews of *The Chronology of Mycenaean Pottery* by Arne Furumark and *The Mycenaean Pottery, Analysis and Classification* by Arne Furumark. *American Journal of Archaeology* 47: 252-54.

Dikaios, Porphyrios
1969
Enkomi. Excavations 1948-1958, I: *The Architectural Remains. The Tombs.* Mainz.

1971
Enkomi. Excavations 1948-1958, II: *Chronology, Summary and Conclusions.* Mainz.

Forbes, R. J.
1964
Studies in Ancient Technology, VIII. Leiden.

Gjerstad, Einar
1926
Studies on Prehistoric Cyprus. Uppsala.

Hult, Gunnel
1978
"Excavations in Area 8 in 1974 and 1975." *Hala Sultan Tekke* 4. Göteborg.

Petrie, William Matthew Flinders
1923
The Arts and Crafts of Ancient Egypt. London.

Robinson, D. M.
1940
"Haus." Pauly-Wissowa, *Real-Encyclopädie der klassischen Altertumswissenschaft.* Supplement 7: 252-78.

Taylor, Joan du Plat
1952
"A Late Bronze Age Settlement at Apliki." *Antiquaries' Journal* 32: 133-44.

Vermeule, Emily T.
1974
Toumba tou Skourou. Boston.

Walters, H. B.
1900
"Excavations at Curium." A. S. Murray, H. B. Walters, and A. H. Smith, *Excavations in Cyprus.* London. 57-86.

Weinberg, Saul S.
1952
"Kourion-Bamboula: The Late Bronze Age Architecture." *American Journal of Archaeology* 56: 178.

ILLUSTRATIONS

FIGURE 1

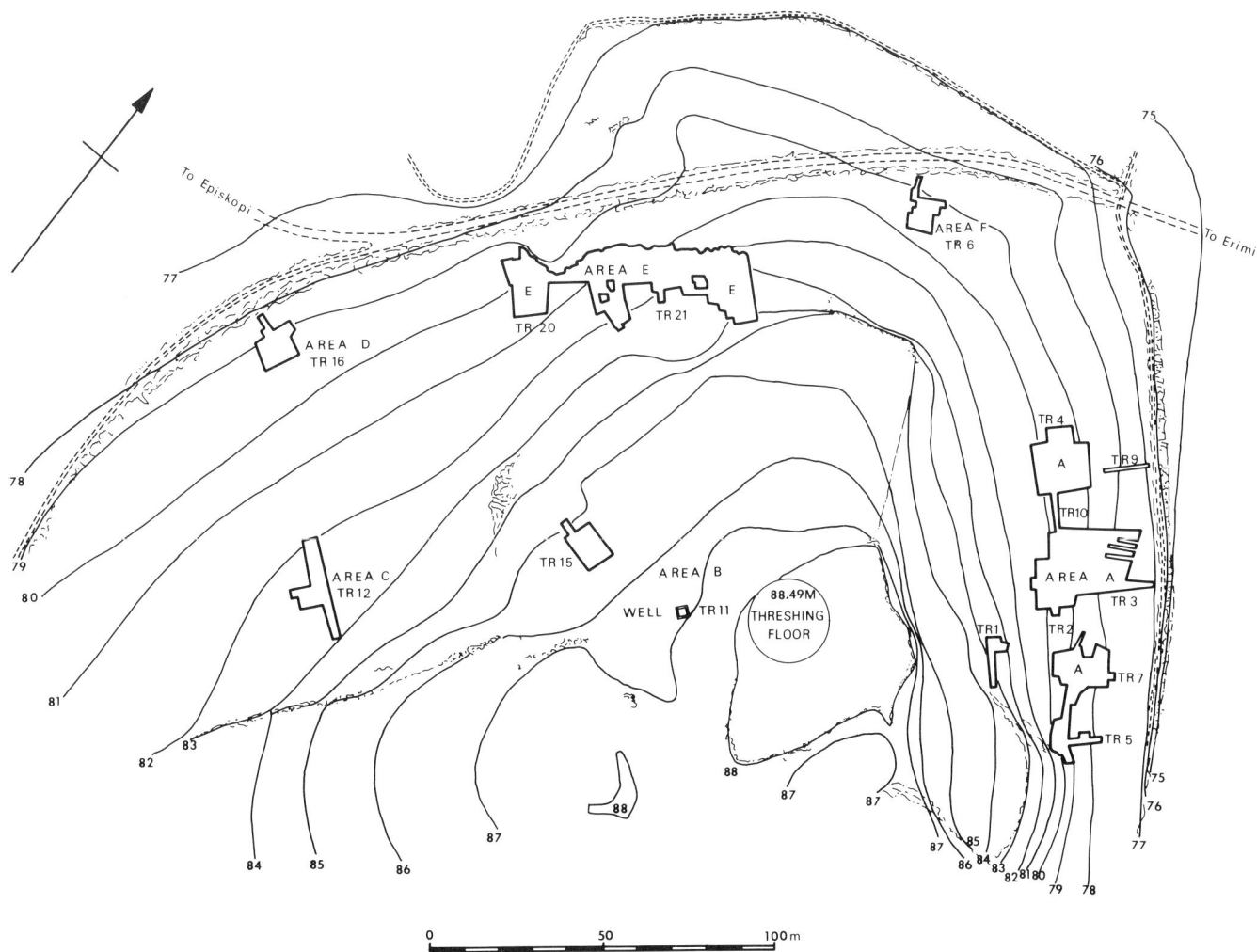

Figure 1. Plan of Kourion-Bamboula. 1:2000.

FIGURE 2

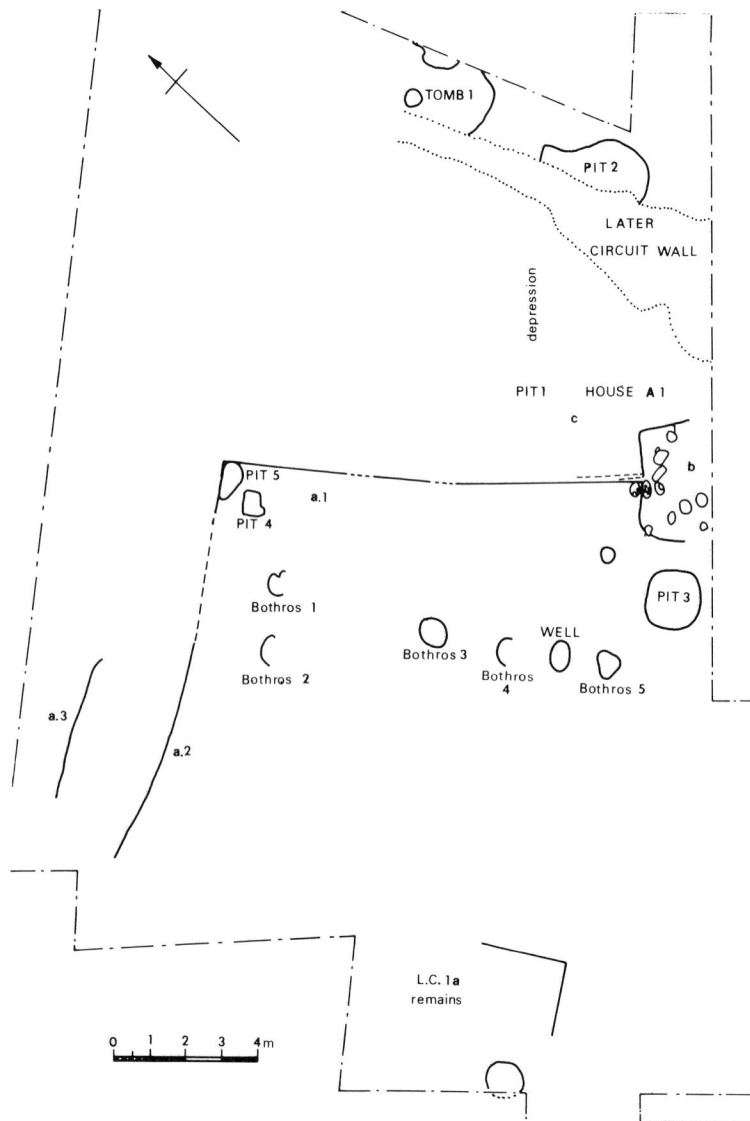

Figure 2. Plan of Stratum A, Area A. 1:200.

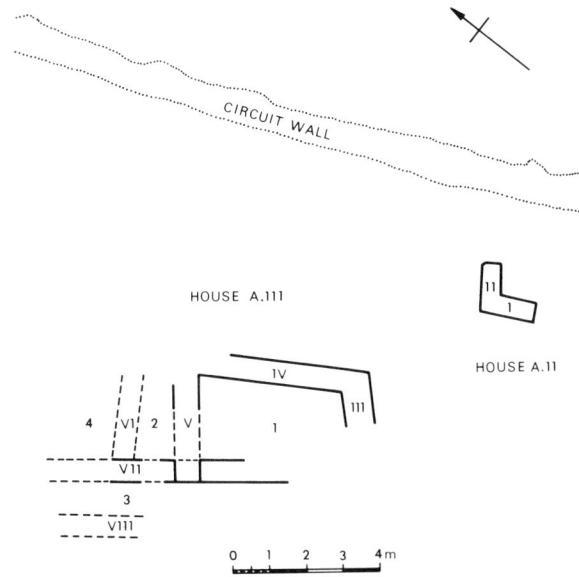

Figure 3. Plan of Stratum B, Area A. 1:200.

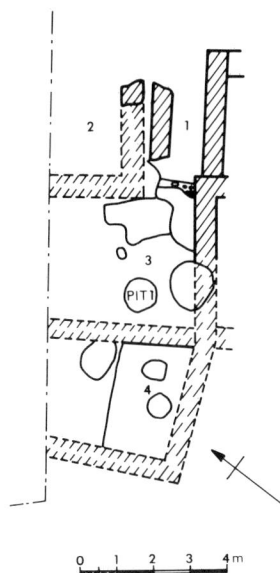

Figure 4. Reconstructed plan of House A.IV. 1:200.

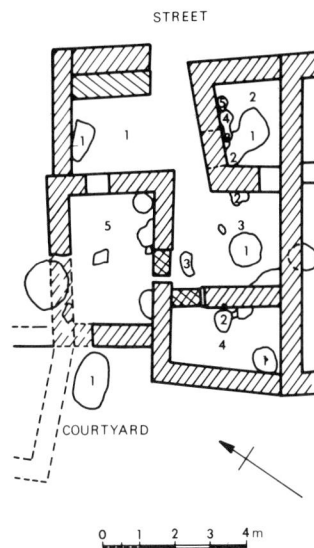

Figure 5. Reconstructed plan of House A.V. 1:200.

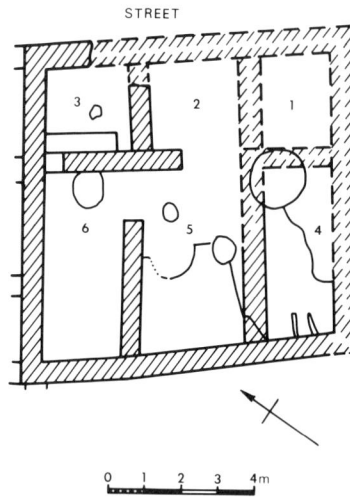

Figure 6. Reconstructed plan of Period D, House A.VI. 1:200.

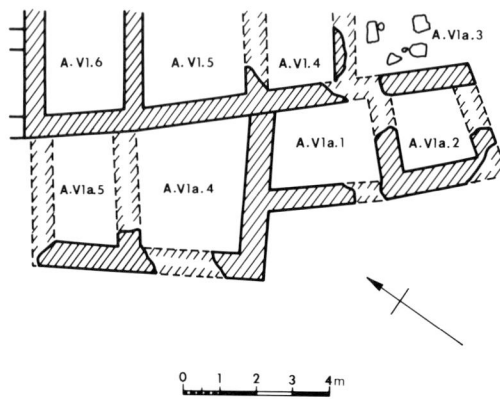

Figure 7. Reconstructed plan of House A.VIa. 1:200.

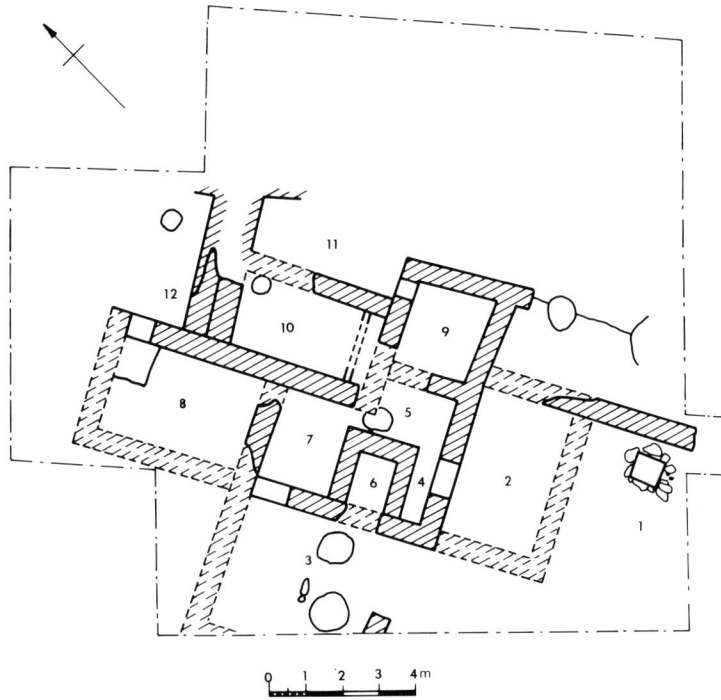

Figure 8. Reconstructed plan of Trench 4, House A.VII. 1:200.

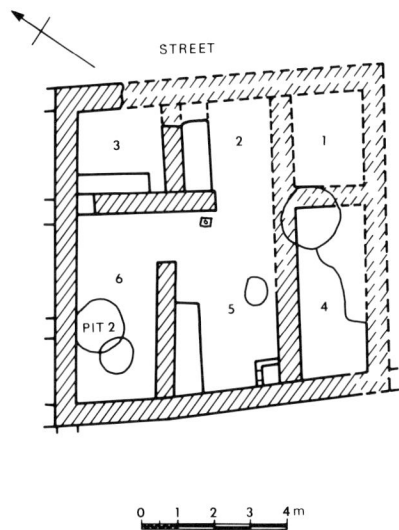

Figure 9. Reconstructed plan of Stratum E, House A.VI. 1:200.

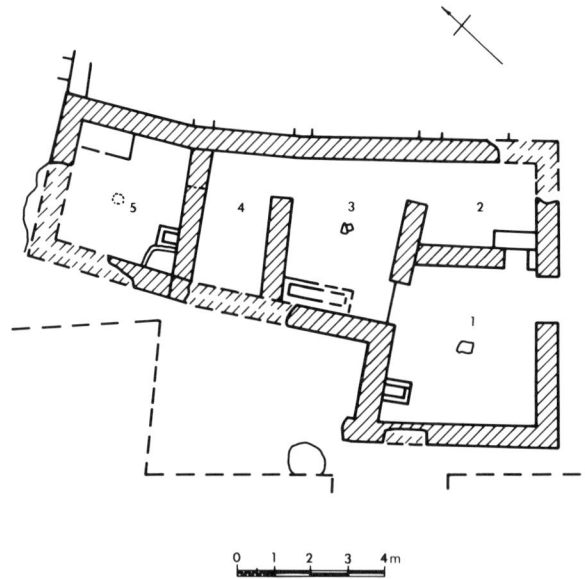

Figure 10. Reconstructed plan of House A.VIII. 1:200.

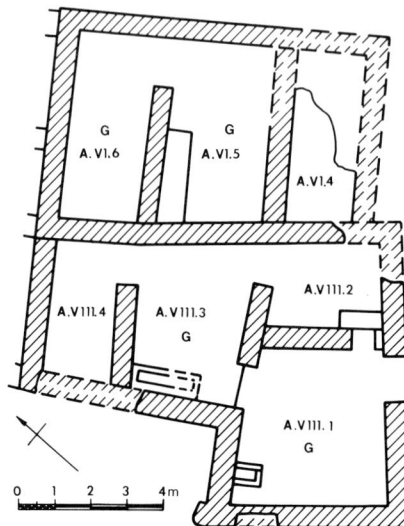

Figure 11. Reconstructed plan of Strata F and G, Area A. G = Remains of Stratum G.
1:200.

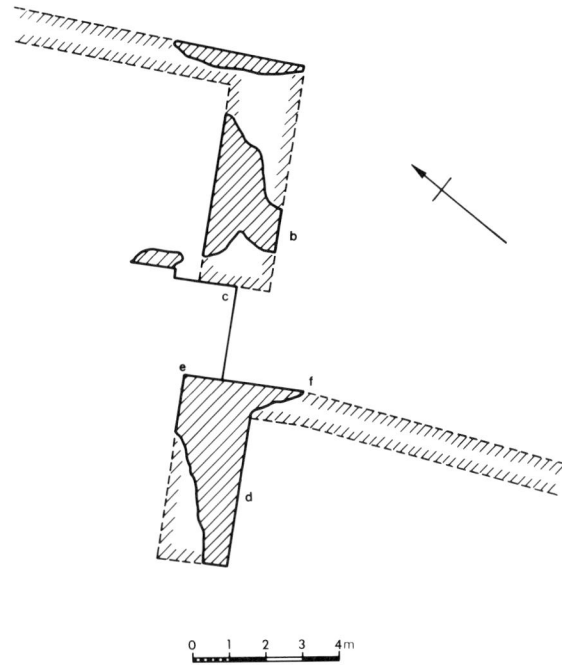

Figure 12. Reconstructed plan of Late Cypriote Gate, Circuit Wall, Area A. 1:200.

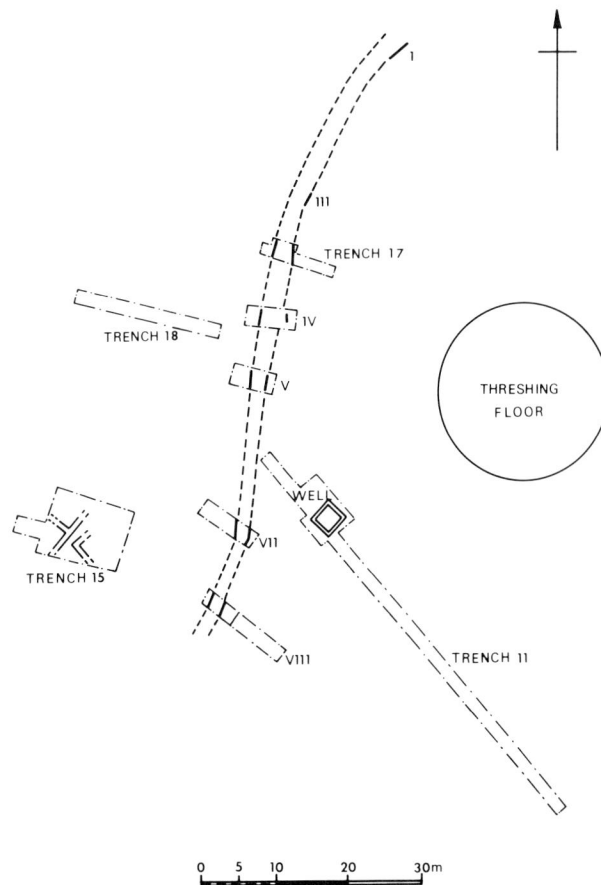

Figure 13. Plan of Area B, Kourion-Bamboula. 1:1000.

Figure 14. Plan of Trench 15, Area B. 1:200.

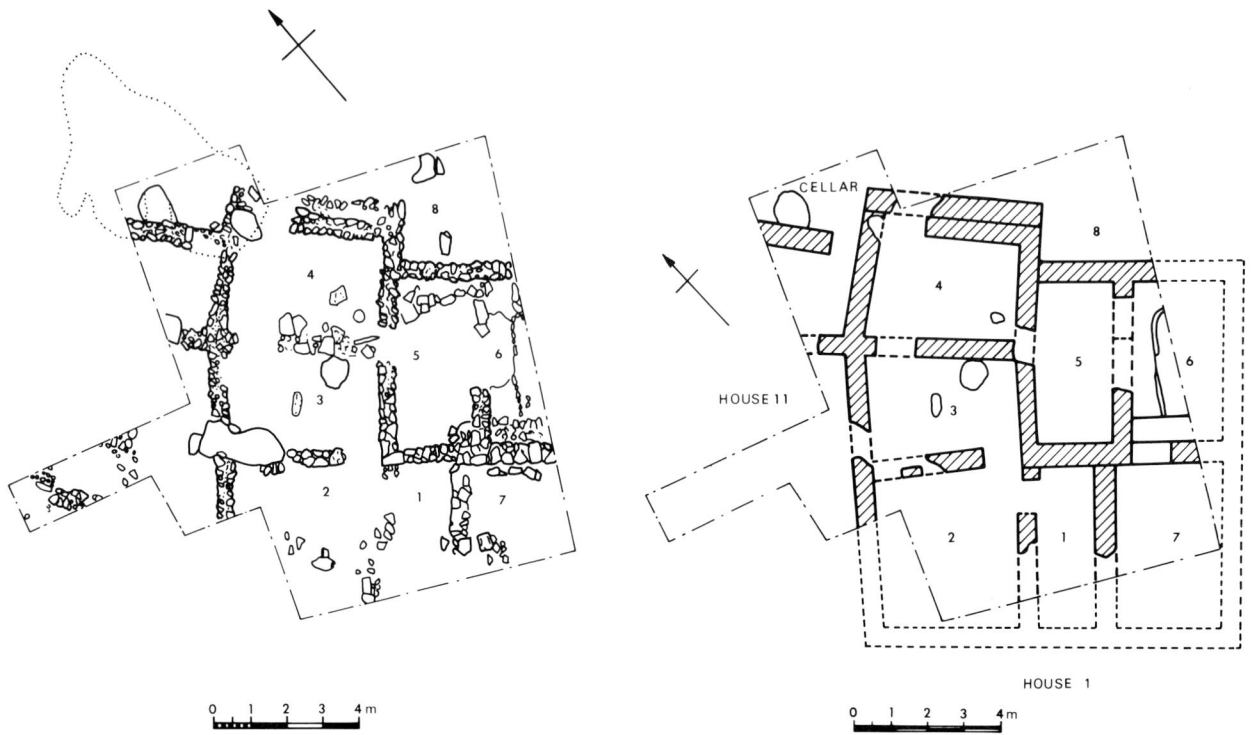

Figure 15. Plan of Trench 16, Area D. 1:200.

Figure 16. Reconstructed plan of Area D, House 1. 1:200.

FIGURE 17

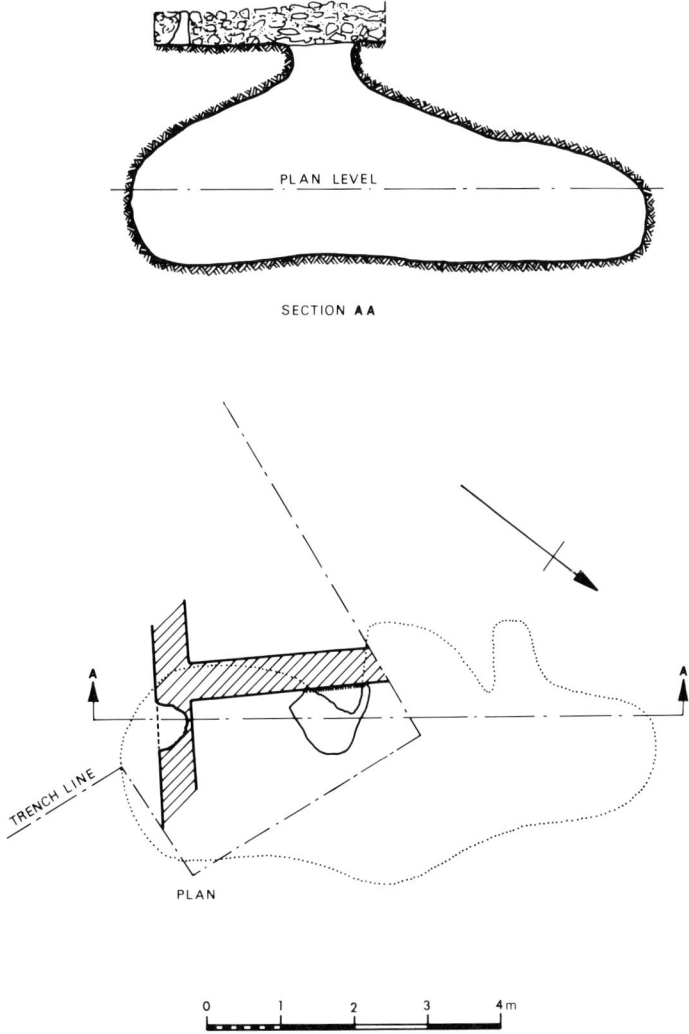

PLAN LEVEL

SECTION **A A**

TRENCH LINE

PLAN

0 1 2 3 4 m

Figure 17. Plan and section of Cellar, Area D. 1:100.

FIGURE 18

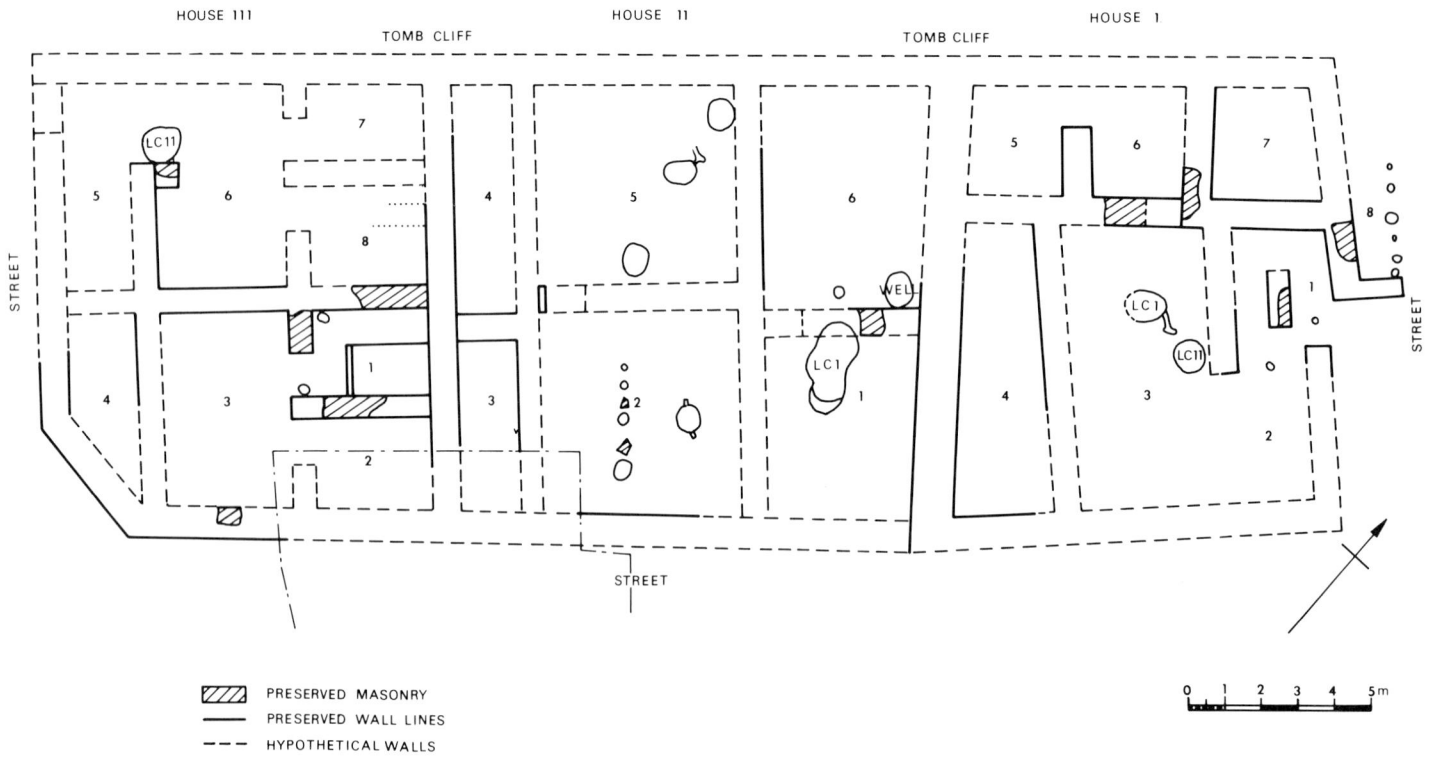

Figure 18. Reconstructed plan of Houses I, II, III, Area E. 1:200.

FIGURE 19

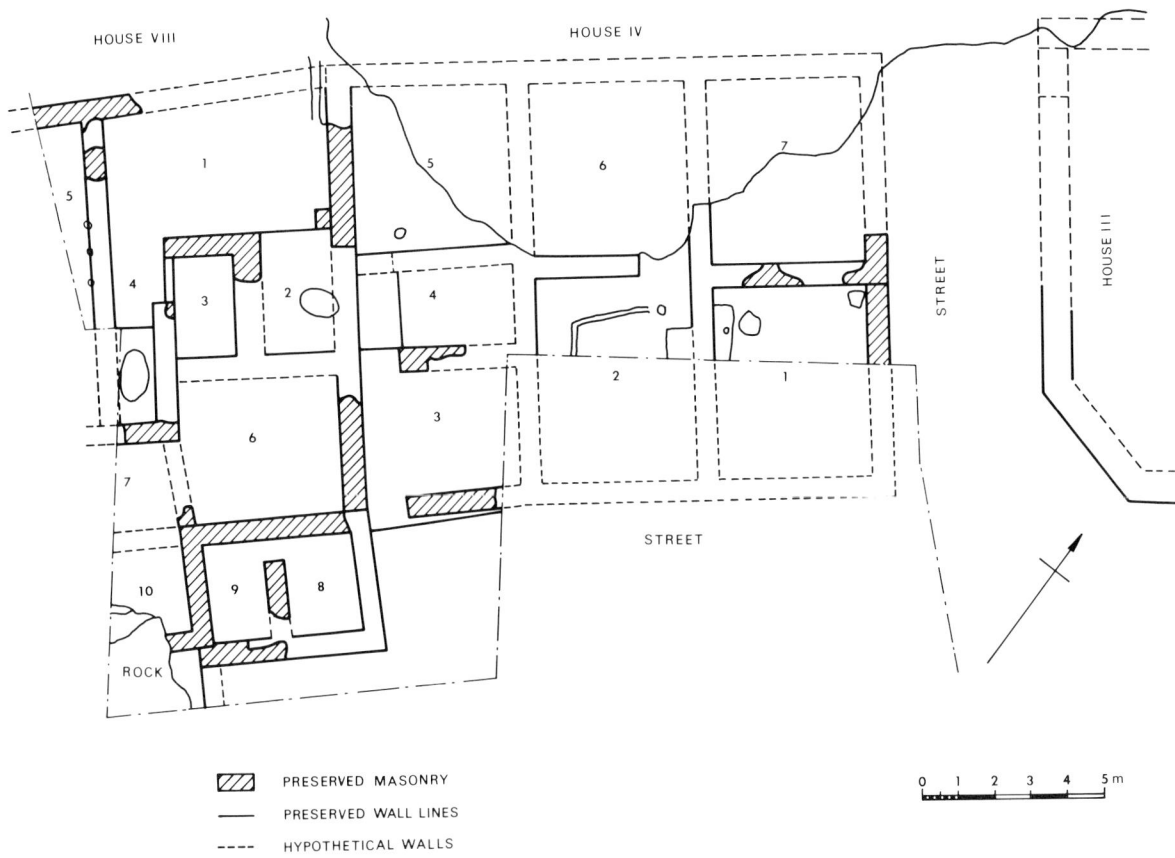

Figure 19. Reconstructed plan of Houses IV, VIII, Area E. 1:200.

FIGURE 20

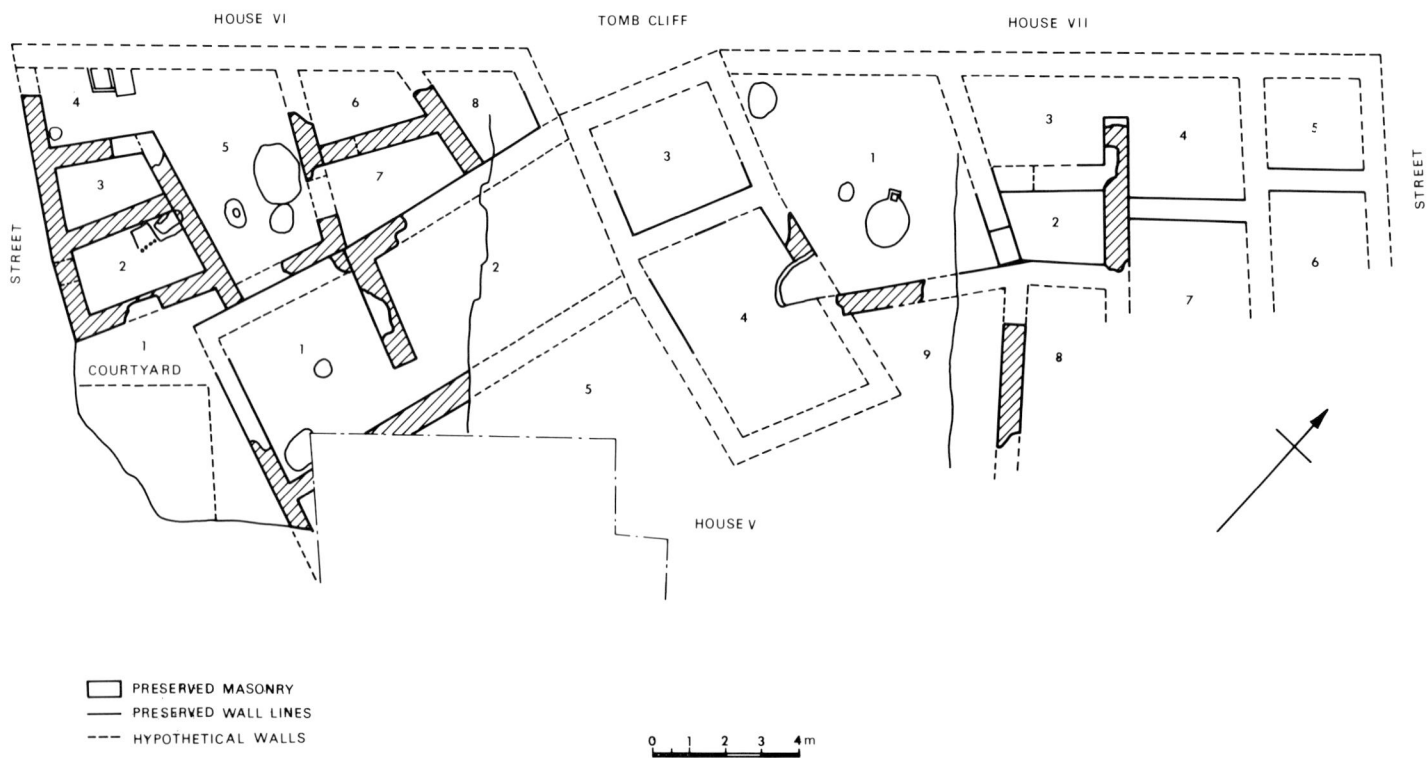

Figure 20. Reconstructed plan of Houses V, VI, VII, Area E. 1:200.

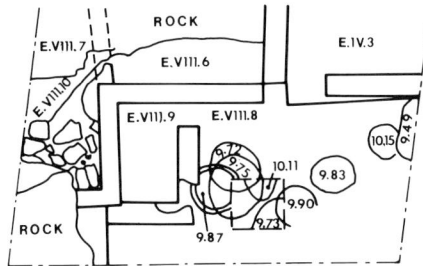

Figure 21. Plan of the Hearth Area, Area E. 1:200.

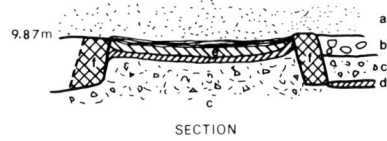

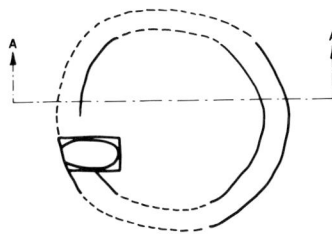

Figure 22. Plan and sectional view of Hearth at −9.87 m., Area E. 1:50.

FIGURE 23

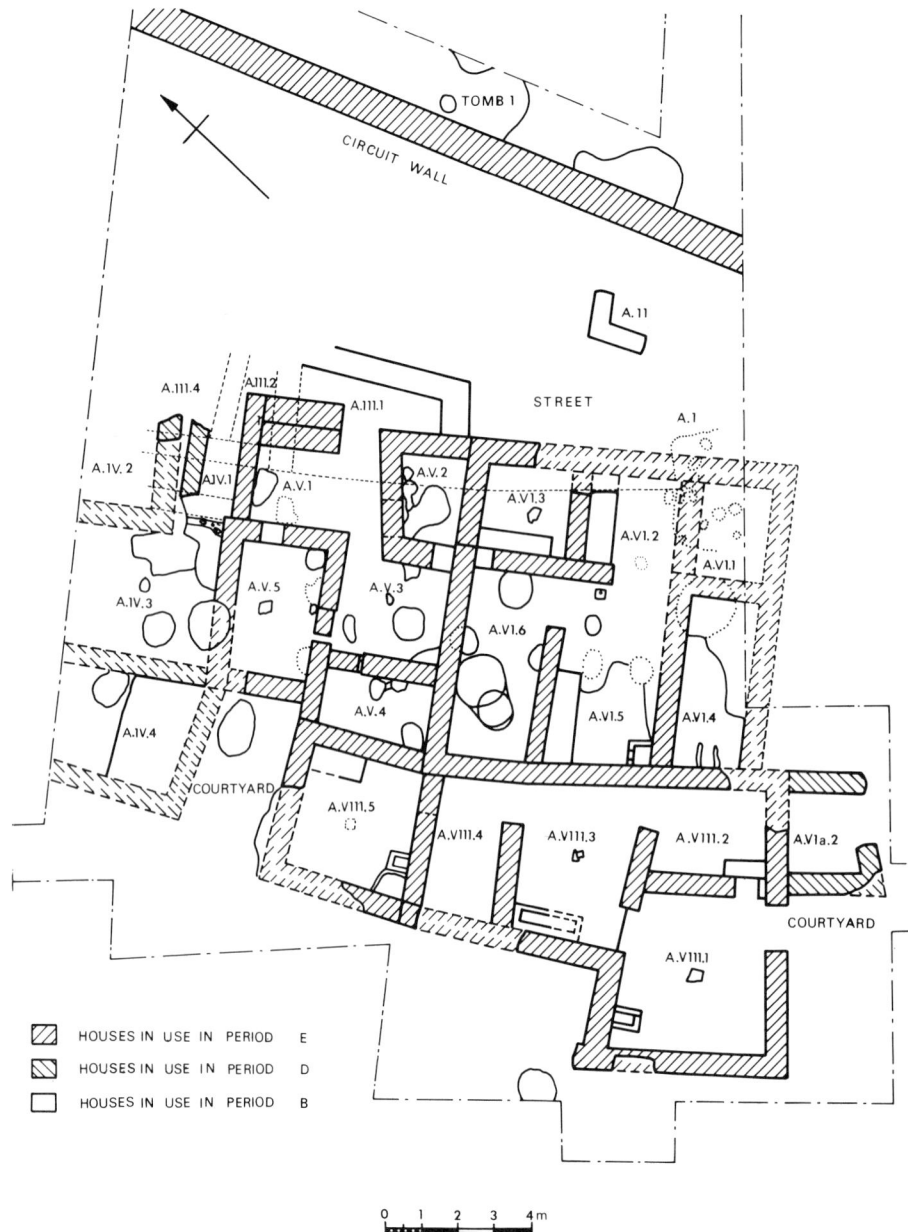

Figure 23. Reconstructed plan of House Complex, Area A. 1:200.

PLATE 1

a. View of Bamboula from northwest.

b. Area A, Tomb 1 from south.

PLATE 2

a. House A.IV from southwest.

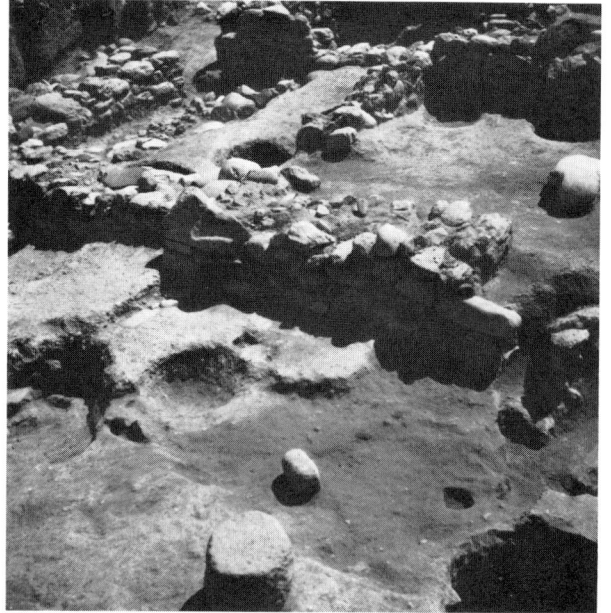

b. House A.IV.3 from west.

c. House A.IV.4 from east.

d. House A.V.5 from northwest.

PLATE 3

a. House A.VI.4. North corner from east.

b. House A.VI.4. Southwest end from northeast.

c. House A.VI.6. Pit at northeast end of room, from northeast.

d. House A.VIa.3 from southeast.

PLATE 4

a. House A.VII.1. Rectangular shaft from southeast.

b. House A.VII.10. Drain across southeast end, from northeast.

c. House A.VII.5. Objects on floor in southeast half, from northwest.

d. House A.VIII.1 from southeast.

PLATE 5

a. House A.VIII.3. Bench with pit on southwest side, from northwest.

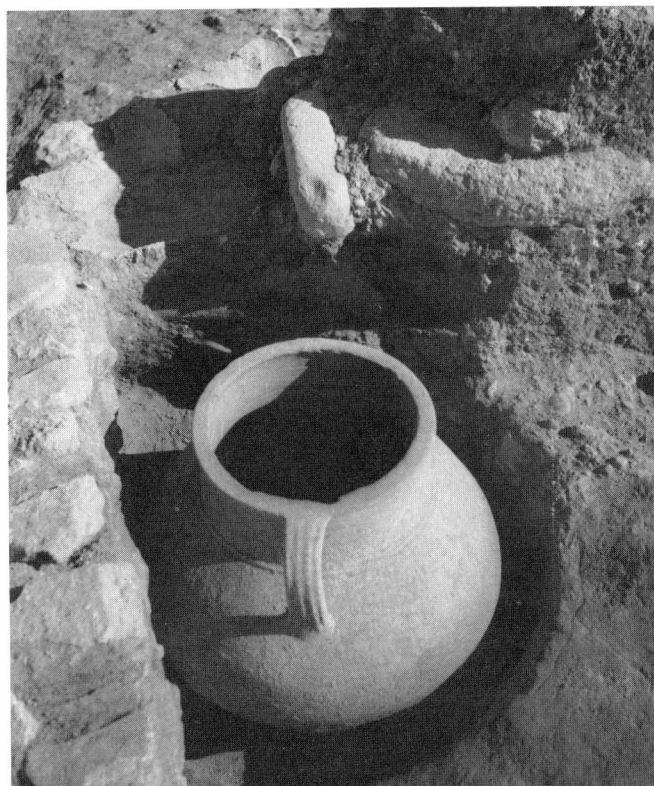

b. House A.VIII.3. Krater in east corner of room, from northwest.

c. House A.VIII.5. Double bin in south corner, from northwest.

PLATE 6

a. Circuit Wall. South end of Archaic and Late Cypriote walls, from southeast.

b. Circuit Wall. Detail of south end of Late Cypriote wall, from southeast.

c. Circuit Wall. Detail of south end of Archaic wall, from southeast.

d. Circuit Wall. Brick staircase from northwest.

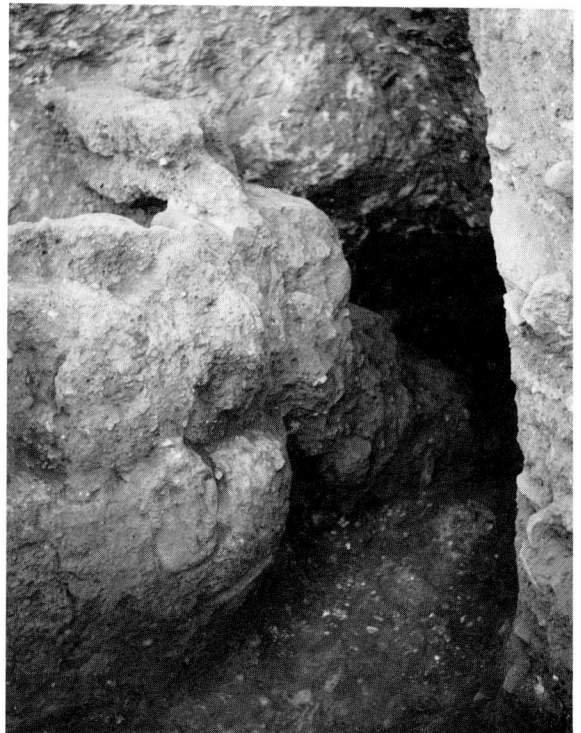

e. Circuit Wall. Brick staircase from north.

PLATE 7

a. Circuit Wall. Two towers from northeast.

b. Circuit Wall. Northeast wall and tower from northwest.

c. Circuit Wall. Detail of northeast wall of northeast tower, from north, showing Late Cypriote face above, Archaic face below.

d. Circuit Wall. Central section from southeast.

e. Circuit Wall. Early stone mass within southwest tower, from southwest.

f. Circuit Wall. Early stone mass within northeast tower, from southwest.

PLATE 8

a. Well in Area B showing upper portion as found, from south-southwest.

b. Well in Area B. View of interior showing built stone walls.

c. Well in Area B. Stone with rope cuttings.

d. Well in Area B as reconstructed, from southeast.

PLATE 9

a. House D.I.5 and 6 from northeast.

b. House D.I.4 from northwest, showing orthostates.

c. House D.I.4 from northwest, showing double northeast wall.

d. House D.II with entrance to cellar.

e. Area E. Panoramic view from north.

PLATE 10

a. House E.I.4. Pavement of large pebbles.

b. House E.I.4. Detail of pebble floor.

c. House E.II, showing rock cutting for wall with House E.I.

d. House E.III.1 with floor of potsherds.

PLATE 11

a. Street of Tombs from northeast.

b. House E.IV.1, 7 and 2 from northeast.

c. House E.IV.2 from northeast.

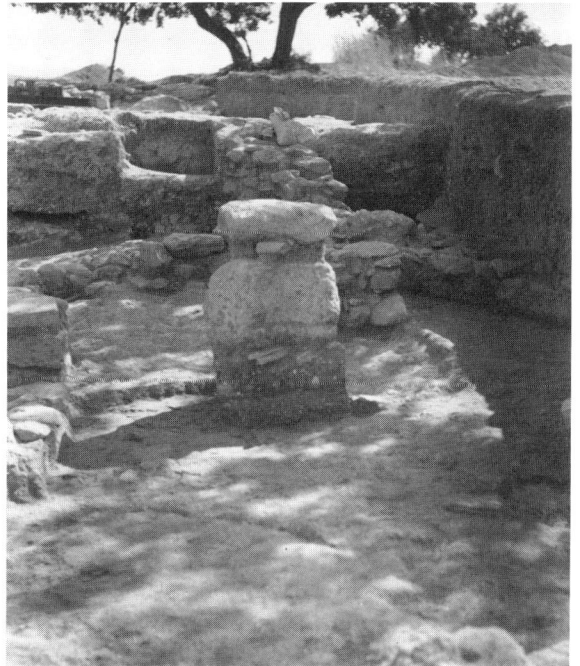
d. House E.IV.3-5 from southeast

e. House E.V.1 from southwest.

PLATE 12

a. House E.V.3-4, showing rock cutting for wall, from north.

b. House E.V.4 with floor of potsherds and pebbles, from east.

c. House E.VI from south.

d. House E.VI.2 with oven and pit, from southwest.

e. House E.VI.2 and 7 from east. Closed door between Rooms 7 and 6 in upper left.

PLATE 13

a. House E.VII.2 and 3 from southwest, across E.VII.1.

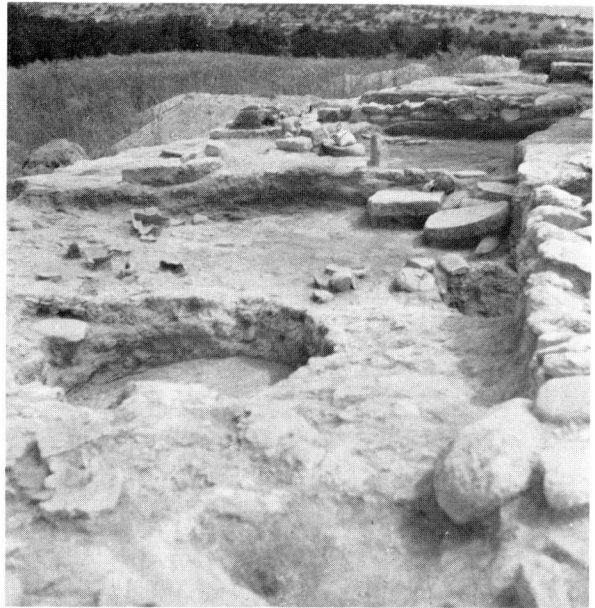

c. House E.VIII.1, 2 and 3 from west.

b. House E.VII.1 from southwest.

d. House E.VIII. View across Room 4 to 3 and 2, from southwest.

PLATE 14

a. House E.VIII. Threshold between Rooms 3 and 4, from southeast.

c. House E.VIII.10, south end from north.

d. Large block on rock-cut foundation for party wall between E.I and E.II.

b. House E.VIII.8 from northeast.

e. Episkopi. Modern house roof with beams and matting to support clay; view from below.